Medical Records Review and Analysis

Medical Records Review and Analysis

Charles C. Sharpe

Auburn House
Westport, Connecticut • London

Library of Congress Cataloging-in-Publication Data

Sharpe, Charles C., 1935–
Medical records review and analysis / Charles C. Sharpe.
p. cm.
Includes bibliographical references and index.
ISBN 0–86569–283–1 (alk. paper)
1. Medical records—Law and legislation—United States.
2. Physicians—Malpractice—United States. I. Title.
KF3827.R4S48 1999
344.73'0412—dc21 98–47758

British Library Cataloguing in Publication Data is available.

Library of Congress Catalog Card Number: 98–47758
ISBN: 0–86569–283–1

First published in 1999

Auburn House, 88 Post Road West, Westport, CT 06881
An imprint of Greenwood Publishing Group, Inc.
www.greenwood.com

Printed in the United States of America

The paper used in this book complies with the Permanent Paper Standard issued by the National Information Standards Organization (Z39.48–1984).

P

In order to keep this title in print and available to the academic community, this edition was produced using digital reprint technology in a relatively short print run. This would not have been attainable using traditional methods. Although the cover has been changed from its original appearance, the text remains the same and all materials and methods used still conform to the highest book-making standards.

Contents

Preface

This book was originally conceived as a handbook for paralegals and other legal assistants collaborating with attorneys in prosecuting cases of medical or nursing malpractice. In the health care environment of today, it will also serve as a reference for laypersons in the event that they, or members of their family, might be victims of an alleged incident of malpractice, and they elect to obtain and review their own or, where authorized, another's medical record.

The basic concepts, principles, and guidelines presented also apply to other areas of personal injury such as accidents and also to workers' compensation claims, toxic torts, medical insurance claims, product liability, disability claims, and criminal cases.

The book includes a discussion of the fundamentals of malpractice. This material is presented as an introduction for the layperson and as a review for the paralegal. This is not a textbook on the law, and I disclaim any intention of offering the reader legal advice. That is the sole prerogative of a member of the legal profession in an attorney-client relationship. In presenting this informational material, I have endeavored to avoid "legalese" and technical language. A glossary of common legal terms, which may be encountered in the area of malpractice law, has been included for the convenience of the layperson.

I have deliberately avoided the inclusion of technical and scientific material on anatomy, physiology, laboratory tests, and medical and nursing procedures, treatments, and equipment. Should a reviewer encounter a specific question in any of these areas, there are a vast array of current and authoritative resources available in libraries and on the Internet.

Missing also are legal citations of cases and court decisions. I consider these to be largely irrelevant in the process of review and analysis of an individual medical record. They would likely prove of no great value to a layperson. My objective is to advise the reader on what to look for and where to look for it—how to evaluate what is presented in the documents in a medical record and, most important, how to determine what is *not* presented and its possible significance to a case.

Members of the paralegal profession are advised to consider the discussion of telemedicine in chapter 13. To date, very little is being said about this topic in the textbooks and curricula of paralegal education. I encourage you to think about the emerging challenges that telemedicine will present to the legal profession, to the health care profession, and to the American people as consumers of their services.

Medical Records Review and Analysis

1

Review of the Medical Record in Cases of Personal Injury and Malpractice

THE EVENTS THAT REQUIRE A REVIEW OF A MEDICAL RECORD

A claim of or a lawsuit for medical malpractice will be the single most common event that will motivate an attorney (or the injured party) to obtain a patient's medical record and undertake a detailed review and analysis of it. The need will also arise in other incidents of personal injury, in claims for workers' compensation or disability, toxic torts, or product liability. The focus of this book and of the guidelines for review and analysis of a medical record will be on medical malpractice.

DEFINITION OF MALPRACTICE

Malpractice is a tort of negligence. It is negligence on the part of a professional when—and only when—such an individual is acting in such a capacity and is carrying out duties for which certain levels of knowledge, skills, and standards are required of any one assuming those duties. It is a failure to act in accordance with those standards. It is a failure to foresee those consequences that any individual in the same position, having similar knowledge, education, and skills, should have foreseen. It is the breach of a professional duty to act in good faith and with reasonable care. Any individual can be liable for negligence, but only a professional can be sued for and found liable (not "guilty") for malpractice.

Negligence

Negligence is carelessness. An unintentional tort of negligence results when any person fails in his or her duty of due care and that failure causes injury to another. The negligent individual does not intend the consequences of his or her action, or failure to act, or does not anticipate the consequences. This distinguishes negligence from intentional tort.

"Ordinary" negligence is defined as a deviation from those standards that any reasonable, prudent person should or would apply in the same or similar circumstances. "Gross" negligence (a claim made in a demand for punitive damages) is based on a wanton disregard for the rights or well-being of another person, even when an injury to that person is highly likely, if not certain, to result from the action. It is a deliberate, reckless, and intentional failure to act as any reasonable, prudent person would or should act. Generally, lawsuits for negligence and for malpractice will involve many of the same elements.

THE REQUIRED ELEMENTS OF MALPRACTICE

In reviewing a medical record in a case of alleged malpractice, the attorney, paralegal, or layperson must be able to identify the *four* elements that, under law, are required to prove malpractice—or any other tort of negligence. In order to find the defendant liable, *each* of these four elements must usually be proven by the plaintiff. (An exception is the doctrine of *res ipsa loquitur*, which will be defined in a later section). The plaintiff must present to the jury a *preponderance of evidence* that demonstrates that all of their allegations are more probably true than not. The four required elements of malpractice are: (1) duty, (2) breach of duty, (3) injury, and (4) causation.

Duty

Duty is a legally recognized relationship that has been established between one person and another. If there is no such relationship, there is no duty. This is a basic principle in Anglo-American law. Inherent in duty is the obligation of *due care* that is owed by one individual to another. Due care is that which is dictated by the circumstances or by law.

Duty also embodies the basic legal principle of personal accountability. Each and every human being has an obligation to act in such a way as not to injure another human being. Freedom to act is restricted to the degree that our actions do not intrude upon or violate the rights of others or cause harm to others. Duty requires appropriate, prudent, and reasonable behavior and the exercise of all possible care in avoiding any unreasonable risk to another.

Health care providers in their relationships with patients inevitably establish duties that could present possible cause for a lawsuit. These are established whenever a health care institution or individual practitioners commences the care and treatment of any person who requires or requests their services and who then becomes their patient. Professional duty—the provider-patient relationship—is established when the practitioner initiates any form of medical or nursing treatment or intervention.

The required element of duty is usually not a point at issue in a malpractice case. The documented event of a person having been treated in a hospital or in a physician's office demonstrates duty. A patient's having been admitted to the hospital, assigned a room and a bed, and that members of the medical and nursing staff undertook and continued the medical and nursing care of that patient establishes duty. The very fact that there is a medical record of the care of that patient evidences duty.

If a patient/plaintiff can not demonstrate that a legally recognizable provider-patient relationship existed at the moment of his or her alleged injury, he or she may have no basis on which to make a successful claim of malpractice. He or she must first prove that the health care provider named as defendant owed them a professional duty of care. If the plaintiff can not prove this, he or she may not have a case. The defendant may claim that no such duty existed. Once the plaintiff has established the existence of duty, he or she must then prove that there was a breach of that duty.

Breach of Duty

The second element that must be proven in a case of malpractice is breach of duty. Breach of duty is defined as a *failure in the standards of care.* The plaintiff must prove that the defendant did not carry out the responsibilities of his or her profession or position in the manner prescribed, expected, and appropriate for the particular time, place, and circumstances.

At a deposition or eventual trial, the applicable standards and the scope of practice will be *presented and interpreted* by the plaintiff's or defendant's expert witnesses. They are *not established or defined* by an expert witness. That is the prerogative of a particular profession and the various states in their statues, rules, or regulations. (For a discussion of nursing standards of care, the reader is referred to Sharpe 1999, chapter 4.)

The standards presented by the experts will be compared to those applied by the defendant in the alleged event of malpractice. At issue will be what were the accepted standards of care *contemporaneous* with the alleged incident, and if, and how, they might have been breached by the defendant. "In theory, establishing the standard of care and establishing the breach of that standard are legally separate. In reality, unless there is a factual question about what the defendant did, the proof of the standard of care also proves the defendant's breach" (Richards and Rathbun 1993, 131).

A concept inherent in breach of duty, "foreseeability," follows.

FORESEEABILITY

Another intrinsic element in malpractice lawsuits is foreseeability. This proposes that any reasonable, prudent person of ordinary intelligence should be able to realize, and predict, the nature and extent of the possible or probable consequences of his or her actions or omissions. One should be able to appreciate the fact that a given action or course of action can be expected to produce given results. Any *predictable* harm that resulted from the absence of due care on his or her part should have been readily foreseen.

Proving foreseeability requires the patient/plaintiff to show that practitioners should have reasonably foreseen the outcome of their actions, given the circumstances surrounding the alleged incident at that time. Such proof cannot come from hindsight; it must be based on the providers' perspective at the time of the event, not the patient/plaintiff's retrospective after the fact. In law, the general rule is that if the consequences were not foreseeable by a reasonable person, there is no liability.

Injury

The third required element is that of injury ("injury in fact"), which is an *actual* harm of any kind—physical, emotional, or economic—that the plaintiff must prove that he or she has suffered. The primary purpose of the law of torts is to provide some form of compensation to the person who has been harmed in any way by a wrongful act of someone else. The harm suffered by the plaintiff must be "compensable"—it must be a *legally recognizable* injury. *Injury is the key element in proving malpractice.* If the plaintiff can not prove injury, there is nothing compensable. Therefore, there is no malpractice, and there can be no liability on the part of the practitioner—even if he or she was negligent!

Incurrence of an injury does not necessarily create liability. This arises only when the injury is the result of a breach of duty. Any patient may fall, suffer a severe adverse reaction to a medication, or not survive a high-risk surgical procedure. These events inevitably happen, and if and when they are unforeseen, unavoidable, accidental, there may be no liability as a result.

A plaintiff's claim of emotional harm may not be sustainable where there is no presenting evidence of serious physical injury. Depending on the jurisdiction, the courts may not allow lawsuits based on such claims. An exception may be where it can be demonstrated that the actions of the defendant were outrageous, extreme, or grossly negligent. A plaintiff has the right to sue for psychological harm; however, courts in many jurisdictions have not been willing to award damages for such claims. In a court case in Pennsylvania, the judge opined that the legal system is not charged with compensating for "every minor psychic shock incurred in the course of everyday life; the law is not the guarantor of an emotionally peaceful life and cannot protect any of us from the emotional slings and arrows of daily living" (*Pennsylvania Jury Verdicts* 1993, 17).

Causation

In order for a plaintiff to prove this fourth element in malpractice, he or she must show that there was a *causal connection* between the breach of duty that is claimed and the alleged injury. He or she must demonstrate the principle of cause and effect that states that a given action or combination of actions will produce a given result. In law this is known as the "but for" principle—but for the action (or omission) of the defendant, the plaintiff's injury would not have occurred. The plaintiff will be required to establish *causation in fact*—that is, the defendant's act was the *proximate* and *substantial* cause of the plaintiff's injury. The plaintiff will assert that breach of duty on the part of the defendant is the most likely and probable cause-in-fact of an injury that otherwise would not or could not have occurred.

An assertion of "proximate cause" (legal cause) will be allowed if it can be demonstrated that the action by the defendant was the substantial cause, the "next" cause, of the plaintiff's injury, which was the natural, continuous result of the defendant's negligence. Proximate cause requires determination of foreseeable consequences. Foreseeability, as discussed previously, is the standard test for proximate cause. A plaintiff will recover damages only if he or she can show that the defendant should reasonably have foreseen that, as a likely consequence of his or her action, the plaintiff was at risk for injury.

THE DOCTRINE OF *RES IPSA LOQUITUR*

This legal doctrine can be an exception to the requirement that a plaintiff must prove all four of the required elements of malpractice. *Res ipsa loquitur* translates literally from Latin as: "The thing for itself speaks." It is the *inference* of the defendant's negligence based on presenting incontestable evidence. The courts developed this concept to apply to those situations in which a definitive act of negligence can not be shown, yet it is patently obvious that there was an injury and that it could only have been caused by an act of negligence.

When invoked as a legal principle and used as a rule of evidence, the doctrine proposes that a defendant's negligence can be *inferred* from the very fact that there was some action on his or her part that caused a readily apparent injury to the plaintiff. The obviousness, the very nature and degree of the plaintiff's injury may infer negligence by the defendant and, therefore, liability. Generally, the doctrine is applied only when the plaintiff's injury is such that it could ordinarily not occur except as a result of negligence.

The prosecution will claim that a duty of care existed, that negligence was the most likely cause of the injury, and that the defendant had *exclusive control* over the events that caused the injury. The burden of proof then shifts to the defense who will endeavor to show that the plaintiff's injury was the result of one or more other causes, rather than negligence on the part of the defendant.

In a malpractice lawsuit, the element of causation can be the most problematic one of the four. In those instances where a number of individuals are named as defendants, a plaintiff may be unable to prove a claim of negligence by any particular one. In such situations, a court may allow *res ipsa loquitur* to assist the plaintiff. In effect, the court attempts to level the playing field by introducing a measure of equality that had been denied the plaintiff. It does this by permitting the plaintiff to attempt to prove a claim by presenting circumstantial evidence against the defendants—any one of whom may know the exact cause of the plaintiff's injury.

Before applying the rule of *res ipsa loquitur*, the court will require that three conditions be met:

1. Given the circumstances surrounding the event, there is reasonable cause to believe that the plaintiff's injury could not have otherwise occurred unless there had been negligence on the part of the defendant.
2. The mode, the instrumentality, of the injury was under the exclusive control of the defendant.
3. The plaintiff did not contribute to the injury in any way. There was no comparative negligence on the part of the plaintiff.

When the doctrine *res ipsa loquitur* is applied, the plaintiff is usually not required to present the testimony of expert witnesses. (Plaintiffs may attempt to claim *res ipsa loquitur* when they are unable to locate expert testimony to support their allegations.) When it is allowed, the plaintiff no longer has the burden of proving all four of the required elements of malpractice. However, he or she must still prove injury and causation.

COMMON BASES OF MALPRACTICE LAWSUITS

The most common causes of malpractice lawsuits against physicians and nurses are shown in tables 1 and 2.

Table 1
Mean and Median Malpractice Payment Amounts Made for the Benefit of Physicians by Malpractice Reason
(Cumulative: September 1, 1990–December 31, 1997)

Malpractice Reason	Mean Payment	Median Payment
Obstetrics related	$336,521	$175,000
Anesthesia related	$209,604	$ 68,751
Diagnosis related	$206,495	$100,000
Monitoring related	$195,776	$100,000
Treatment related	$166,137	$ 75,000
Surgery related	$152,624	$ 75,000
IV & blood products related	$147,791	$ 75,000
Medication related	$139,561	$ 40,000
Miscellaneous	$ 89,745	$ 25,000
Equipment or product related	$ 70,517	$ 22,750

Source: National Practitioner Data Bank, *Annual Report, 1997,* Table 10.

There are a number of common bases that have been consistently identified as giving rise to malpractice lawsuits against nurses. These can be grouped into seven principal categories shown in table 2.

Table 2
Common Bases of Nursing Malpractice Lawsuits

1. Safety: Incidents of patient falls continue to be a major cause of malpractice suits against nurses who did not recognize possible risk factors and/or failed to take appropriate preventive measures.
2. Medication Administration Errors: Most such errors are the result of failure to follow the basic techniques and guidelines of medication preparation and administration. Parenteral (IV) medications are a primary risk. One or more of the six "rights" had not been observed: the right (1) patient, (2) medication, (3) dose, (4) route, (5) time, and (6) technique.

3. Assessment and Monitoring: Failure to properly monitor, assess, and report a patient's status. This has been identified in a majority of malpractice lawsuits.
4. Procedures and Treatments: Improper or inadequate nursing intervention. Not following the institution's policies and procedures, including risk management principles.
5. Equipment: Misuse, Defect, Failure: Using equipment without proper training. Failure to test equipment before use, and to read instructions, specifications, and warnings. Attempting to repair, adapt, or modify equipment. The increasing use, complexity, and sophistication of medical devices have created innumerable possibilities for injury and liability.
6. Communication: Breakdown in communications between nurse and physician or among other members of the health care team. Failure to report the errors or impairment of others responsible for patient care. Not listening to the patient.
7. Documentation: Inadequate documentation in nurses' notes is a *principal* factor in adverse court decisions in malpractice lawsuits.

Source: Sharpe, 1999, chapter 5.

CORROBORATING MALPRACTICE FROM THE MEDICAL RECORD

In order for a paralegal or, certainly, a layperson to conduct an effective review and analysis of a medical record and produce a meaningful summary, he or she should have an understanding of the basic legal principles of malpractice—the allegation that has placed the medical record in his or her hands. During the course of the review, there should be an attempt to confirm that any or all of the four required elements of malpractice are evident in the record.

It is not the attorney's, the paralegal's, or the layperson's prerogative to determine that the alleged malpractice has, in fact, occurred. They may form such an opinion, and they may assert it in their claims. They can not, however, make a definitive judgment that there has been an act of malpractice. That determination can be made only after expert witnesses have examined the record, corroborated their opinions that there has, or has not, been an incident of malpractice, and presented those opinions to a judge and/or jury who will ultimately make the definitive decision.

DEFENSES IN MALPRACTICE LAWSUITS

In the process of reviewing and analyzing a medical record, the paralegal or lay reviewer must endeavor to identify those documents or entries that could possibly provide a substantive basis for one or more of the possible defenses that may be put forth in a claim of malpractice.

Types of Defenses

There are two principal types of "affirmative" defense that will be put forth in a suit for malpractice. Affirmative defenses are defined in substantive law. Specific affirmative defenses will be offered based on the type of tort that forms the basis of the lawsuit. They will be presented in an effort to demonstrate that there were certain facts or circumstances that preclude the claims of the plaintiff. These defenses do not deny the truth or facts of the plaintiff's claims. Rather they contend that the defendant is not liable for the various reasons stated. They challenge the plaintiff's legal right to bring the action against the defendant. The two types are (1) defense of fact and (2) defense in law. The review of the medical record may or may not offer corroborative evidence of a defense.

Defense of Fact

The defendant's attorney will contend that there was, in fact, no breach of duty; or they will concur that there was a breach of duty, but that it could not have caused the injury alleged by the plaintiff. Any number of other possible causes will be presented as contributing to the injury. The defense will offer a number of possible affirmative defenses including:

- Comparative/contributory negligence: *Both* the patient and the defendant contributed to the injury to some degree. Under this doctrine, a plaintiff may recover damages; however, the amount will be in proportion to the percentage of the plaintiff's proven negligence.
- Assumption of risk: The plaintiff willingly and knowingly accepted the risk of the medical procedure. This was demonstrated by their expressed or implied consent (discussed in chapter 2) or implied by the patient's knowledge of the risks. This defense will claim that the plaintiff was fully aware of and understood all the risks, willingly consented, and in so doing, accepted any and all consequences, including the possibility of the alleged injury.
- Informed consent: The plaintiff voluntarily consented to the procedure. The legal implications of informed consent will be presented in chapter 2.
- Unavoidable accident: An unavoidable and unanticipated event or set of circumstances occurred that caused the injury.

- False claims: The charges and allegations of the plaintiff are so deficient in credibility or proof that they can not sustain the claims.

Defense of Law: Statute of Limitations

A statute of limitations defines the period of time within which a plaintiff is allowed to bring an action in law for malpractice. It is an example of a procedural law. These statutes vary by state. However, in most states the lawsuit must be filed within the prescribed time frame. A statute usually begins to "run" on the specific date on which the plaintiff *knew, should have known,* or *discovered* that a possible incident of malpractice was the likely cause of the alleged injury. If the plaintiff fails to file his or her petition for damages (complaint) within the time frame mandated by the law, he or she could forfeit his or her legal right to bring a lawsuit.

The defendant, in claiming a statute of limitations as a defense, must demonstrate that the statute has, in fact, run. If the court concurs, a plaintiff can not pursue a lawsuit against the defendant. When the specific date on which the statute began to run is an issue, the plaintiff's attorney will try to find any possible extenuating circumstances and will petition the court to extend the statute based on any of these that could be credible.

There are certain procedural rules that a paralegal or lay reviewer should be aware of. The medical record will be a critical source for determining which of these might apply in a particular case of alleged malpractice.

PROCEDURAL RULES IN THE STATUTES OF LIMITATIONS

- Discovery Rule: The statute begins to run on the day the plaintiff discovers that he or she has been injured by an act of malpractice. A court will consider whether or not the plaintiff *could have* or *should have* detected the injury at any time previously. Would this injury have been obvious to any reasonable person?
- Occurrence Rule: The statute begins to run at the instant of the injury.
- Termination-of-Treatment Rule: The statute begins to run on the date of the patient's last treatment.
- Wrongful Death: Statutes dealing with wrongful death usually allow the decedent's survivors, or the executors or administrators of their estate, to file lawsuits claiming malpractice. A court may

determine that the statute begins to run on the date of the patient's death.

- Minors: The statutes of limitations as they apply to minors vary by state. In some it will be defined according to the age of the minor on the date of the sustained injury. There may be no specific provision for minors in some statutes. The rights of parents or legal guardians also varies.
- Fraud: If it can be proven that there was any type of deliberate concealment or deceit on the part of any of the parties to the defense, this could extend the statute of limitations *indefinitely. This definitely includes any attempt to alter or tamper with a medical record*!

Defense of Law: Good Samaritan Laws

Each state has enacted a special statute called a Good Samaritan law that attempts to offer a degree of protection to anyone who attempts to assist a victim at the scene of an accident, disaster, or other emergency situation from claims of negligence. Individual state laws specify those who are covered—including professionals and nonprofessionals. Typically only those persons with a legal duty to rescue as defined by a particular state's law are required to respond in emergencies. These may include paramedics and other emergency medical technicians, fire fighters, police, physicians, and nurses.

Any individual who does respond and attempt to intervene *may be sued*. The Good Samaritan law does not prevent anyone from being sued; however, the law will provide a strong legal defense unless his or her actions have been shown to have been wanton, careless, or grossly negligent. As a general rule, unless required by a particular state's statute, there is *no legal mandate* requiring an individual to render assistance to a victim in an emergency situation. Only two states have such a legal mandate for nurses.

Legal duty is created at the moment that a health care provider initiates medical or nursing intervention and establishes a provider-patient relationship. At that moment the practitioner will be held to the defined standards of care of a particular profession. Legal duty is one of reasonable care, and the Good Samaritan law will protect only the individual who provides such care.

Once the physician or nurse initiates intervention, the victim becomes his or her "patient," and he or she is then required to remain with the victim until released from their legal duty by one of the following events:

- the victim refuses an offer of assistance or requests that the efforts cease;

- the victim is in no imminent danger;
- other qualified personnel arrive on the scene;
- his or her personal safety or life are at risk;
- he or she is directed to leave the scene by a lawful authority;
- he or she is physically unable to continue;
- there is no possible hope of saving the victim.

Good Samaritan laws usually apply only in situations that are encountered outside a health care provider's place of employment. When physicians or nurses are traveling to or from their place of employment or involved in personal activities at home or elsewhere, they are solely responsible for the legal consequences of their actions.

Any practitioners who seek and/or accept any amount of monetary compensation for their rescue efforts on the part of an accident victim could forfeit their rights under a Good Samaritan law. Their actions could be seen as having established a "fee-for-service" situation, which, in effect, is a business arrangement, and which may preclude them from invoking a Good Samaritan defense in the event of litigation.

REFERENCES

Jury Verdict Review Publications. *Pennsylvania Jury Verdicts*. 1993. (October 4).

National Practitioner Data Bank. 1997. United States Department of Health and Human Services, Public Health Service, Health Resources and Service Administration, Bureau of Health Professions. Division of Quality Assurance, National Practitioner Data Bank. *1997 Annual Report*.

Richards, Edward P., and Katharine Rathbun. 1993. *Law and the Physician: A Practical Guide*. Little Brown and Co.

Sharpe, Charles C. 1999. *Nursing Malpractice: Liability and Risk Management*. Auburn House.

2

Legal Implications of Informed Consent and Advance Directives

CONSENT

There have been an increasing number of malpractice lawsuits based on assertions that the plaintiff had not given his or her consent for a treatment or procedure—which may or may not have caused an injury. Two common allegations in claims of malpractice are: (1) battery–the patient claims that he or she did not give *any* form of consent prior to the initiation of the treatment or procedure at issue, or (2) there was a lack of *informed* consent.

Because of the nature and risks of the treatments and procedures for which it is required, informed consent, or lack thereof, is primarily a liability risk for physicians, dentists, or certain other quasi-independent health care providers, such as advanced practice nurses. Various states have enacted both substantive and procedural laws that define informed consent and those claims and defenses that will be allowable and that specify the elements of a claim for a tort of negligent nondisclosure.

When consent is a point at issue, the review of the plaintiff's medical record will involve a search for those particular documents that will confirm or defeat a claim that informed consent was lacking. The paralegal and the lay reviewer should be aware of the basic legal issues in the matter of consent—particularly informed consent. This chapter will discuss what legally constitutes it, the circumstances in which it is required, the responsibility for obtaining it, and the patient's rights in granting or refusing it.

FORMS OF CONSENT

There are two forms of consent that a patient may give. These are "expressed" consent and "implied" consent.

Expressed Consent

Expressed consent is affirmed and declared by the patient personally, either in writing or verbally. In most jurisdictions either form is accepted as valid. In a lawsuit where informed consent becomes the point at issue, proving oral (or implied) consent could present a serious challenge for the defense. If at all possible, a witness should be present for an oral consent, and the details should be documented in the medical record. There should be at least one document in the record attesting consent for routine treatment.

Implied Consent

Implied consent is that which could be inferred from a patient's actions or the inability to act. This would include moving eyes, head, or hands to indicate "yes" or "no" or any other recognizable gesture to express a choice. In those instances where a person is unable to express consent, the law presumes implied consent. The record should have adequate documentation of this form of consent.

DEFINITION OF "INFORMED" CONSENT

Informed consent is that which an individual gives freely and willingly based on the quality and quantity of the information that has been presented to him or her by a health care provider—usually a physician. There can be no coercion or duress of any kind. This includes physical force or psychological pressure in the form of intimidation or threats of any kind. The consent may be given by a patient or by his or her legally appointed surrogate when that is appropriate to the circumstances. It enables a physician, nurse, or other provider of health care—by mutual agreement—to render a service to that person as his or her patient. The act of consent imparts to a practitioner the right to treat that patient—to do something to or for that person that is intended to be therapeutic. Informed consent has evolved from simply obtaining a patient's verbal permission prior to a treatment or procedure into a formal process intended to involve the patient in the personal decision to accept or reject the proposal.

REQUIRED ELEMENTS OF INFORMED CONSENT

The legal standards for informed consent are considerably more complex than the standards that address a complete failure of consent. A lawsuit based on the former will concede that the patient did, in fact, give consent (ruling out charges of battery), but will allege that the patient did not understand the implications of the treatment or procedure to such a degree that he or she was able to make a rational, valid choice.

There are two essential elements required to validate informed consent: (1) legal capacity and (2) the duty of "full disclosure." These are the legal criteria prescribed by virtually all states. However, precisely what a plaintiff may be required to prove to support a claim of negligent nondisclosure may differ from jurisdiction to jurisdiction.

Legal Capacity

Legal capacity may be defined as an individual's ability to fully comprehend all of the implications and consequences of his or her actions. A general rule under the law is that only a person who is considered fully capacitated, or competent, may give valid informed consent—or refuse to give it. Should a plaintiff in a lawsuit claim a lack of informed consent, he or she must show that any reasonable person, in the same or similar circumstances, would not have assented on the basis of the information he or she had received. Any alert, fully oriented adult is normally viewed as capacitated. The patient's *physician* is legally responsible for confirming this status and obtaining informed consent. In some jurisdictions, specified members of a patient's family may give consent when a patient is unable to do so. The patient's spouse would usually be consulted first, then any adult children, and last, a parent. Another essential element is that the consent must be *freely given* by the patient.

Right to Refuse, Revoke, or Withdraw Consent

In 1914, Justice Benjamin Cardozo wrote: "Every human being of adult years and sound mind has a right to determine what shall be done with his own body" (*Schloendorff v. Society of New York Hospital* 211 N.Y. 125, 127, 129; 105 N.E. 92, 93 [1914]). Once the patient has given consent, he or she has the right to withdraw it at any time. This right is not necessarily absolute. The state may supersede in the choice in several instances. Some examples of these are shown below.

INSTANCES IN WHICH RIGHT OF REFUSAL OF CONSENT MAY BE SUPERSEDED

- If the refusal or withdrawal of consent by a parent or guardian would jeopardize the life or well-being of a minor.
- If the individual, by their refusal, unjustifiably jeopardizes their own life.

- If refusal or withdrawal constitutes a threat to the preservation and protection of public health and safety.

Full Disclosure

In examining the consent documents in a medical record, the reviewer will attempt to confirm if there was, in fact, *full* disclosure—the essence of "informed" consent. This is the requirement that *all significant and material facts* be presented to a patient—in *language that he or she can fully understand*—in order that the individual can make an informed decision either to accept or refuse a proposed treatment or procedure. Not *every* conceivable risk or side effect need be presented, but the highest risks and the most adverse possible side effects must be disclosed. This presentation must also include all possible and feasible alternative courses of action—if any. This would include taking no action at all—and the possible consequences of this choice.

Two legal standards are involved in informed consent. The first is that of the "reasonable physician" who must present all of the information that any practitioner would or should under the same or similar circumstances. The second standard is that of the "reasonable patient" who is entitled to all of the information that would be considered necessary for any person in that position to make a rational choice.

Required Elements in Full Disclosure

- A description of the proposed treatment or procedure in language that the patient can comprehend
- All material risks of the procedure—not necessarily each and every risk or possible side effect
- The patient's present clinical status
- Their expected prognosis
- An advisory of possible death or brain injury as a result of the procedure
- Alternative treatments or procedures, if any
- The expected outcome
- An affirmation that there can be no guarantees of success
- A confirmation of the patient's right to refuse and/or revoke their consent at any time
- The likely consequences of a refusal of consent

EXCEPTIONS TO THE NEED FOR INFORMED CONSENT

There are several situations in which a practitioner may not require a patient's informed consent, and therefore, a signed consent document will not be included in the medical record.

- Emergency: The person's life is at immediate risk and there is no time to obtain consent, or the patient is unable to give it.
- Waiver: The patient has waived his or her right to full disclosure.
- Obvious risk: The inherent risks of the treatment or procedure would be known to any reasonable person.
- Therapeutic privilege: The practitioner may reserve the right to withhold any information that he or she considers detrimental to the patient's health or well-being and that could possibly jeopardize the patient's physical or mental status, interfere with treatment, impede recovery, or impair prognosis.
- Extension doctrine: This permits a practitioner to take a course of action that had not been discussed or consented to but that is required by a situation that arises during a procedure.

PROVING LACK OF INFORMED CONSENT

A malpractice lawsuit might not involve any claim by a plaintiff that he or she did not give informed consent for the treatment rendered, or such an assertion can be a peripheral issue. If the lawsuit has its basis in an asserted lack of informed consent, the plaintiff must demonstrate that the physician or other health care practitioner—by their failure in full disclosure—breached their duty to the plaintiff and in so doing caused the plaintiff to decide on a course of action that they would not have elected otherwise. In effect, the patient must prove that this alleged breach of duty was the cause of the injury claimed.

A practitioner's inadvertent deficiency in the requirements of full disclosure may not invalidate the patient's informed consent, but it may become a factor in sustaining a liability claim for negligence. The multitude of laws and the infinite subtleties in interpretation of constituent disclosure factors in informed consent have given rise to many lawsuits.

In most states, a jury will be asked to answer four questions to determine liability:

1. Was the patient provided with the same information that another patient in the same or similar circumstances would usually have been given?

2. Did the patient understand this information to a degree that he or she was able to make a rational choice?
3. Was the patient specifically advised of all of the most significant risks?
4. If any omitted information had been included, would the patient have consented?

If the answer to each of these four questions is "no," the health care provider could be liable for failure to obtain informed consent. The final determination of what a patient should (or need not) have been told under the circumstances will be made by appropriate expert witnesses. Regarding the last question, another difficult question can be raised: Would the information that was omitted have persuaded the patient not to accept the procedure? A jury might assume that, given the fact that the proposed therapy was the most feasible alternative, any reasonable person would have consented to it—regardless.

Damages in Lack of Informed Consent

The determination of damages in these claims can be problematical. "Even if a jury finds the health care provider liable for failure of informed consent, the patient may collect only the actual damages flowing from the accident. A procedure that does the patient no harm will not support a monetary award, despite a finding of failure of informed consent. A successful action for failure of informed consent requires the occurrence of a severe risk that results in a serious injury to the patient. The courts will not accept a suit based on failure of informed consent in the absence of significant harm" (Richards and Rathbun 1983, 426).

WHEN IS INFORMED CONSENT REQUIRED?

The patient's permission for routine, basic nursing and medical procedures is implied by his or her admission to, and very presence in, the hospital. Their request for treatment is tantamount to consent for treatment. During the standard admission process each patient is routinely asked to sign a consent form for those procedures required to provide basic assessments and routine care. During hospitalization, the patient's cooperation in the medical and nursing regimen attests to his or her consent.

For other than routine procedures and treatments, informed consent is required for those that involve a high degree of risk for injury, serious complications, and side effects—or death. This would, of course, include the patient who is to undergo virtually every kind of surgery or high-risk invasive procedure. The individual who is to participate in any experimental treatment or medical trials must give informed consent, which, under federal laws and regulations, has very specific and rigid guidelines.

LEGAL IMPLICATIONS OF FAILURE TO OBTAIN CONSENT

As a general rule, where a treatment or procedure is performed without first obtaining informed consent, a patient can file a successful lawsuit regardless of the outcome of the practitioner's action. Any medical or nursing intervention, or attempts at such intervention, without a competent patient's expressed or implied consent, informed or otherwise, could result in a claim of battery or of negligence in the failure to obtain such consent. Relatively few such cases wind up in criminal courts. Implied consent represented by the patient's seeking medical treatment would usually prevent a claim of battery in most medical care situations. Malpractice litigation that may include a claim of lack of consent is most likely to revolve around a principal issue of professional negligence rather than a minor issue of battery.

"Technical battery" occurs when the actions of a health care provider go beyond the scope of the consent given by a patient. If the patient had revoked his or her consent and the practitioner proceeds in disregard of this revocation, the patient may have a legal right to initiate a lawsuit for battery. The exception could be that the act of withdrawing consent constitutes an immediate and unwarranted risk to the patient's health, well-being, or life itself. Otherwise, the patient has the legal right to refuse.

The right to refuse or to revoke includes a competent patient's election to leave the hospital at any time, for any reason against medical advice (AMA). However, the right of self-discharge is not without limitations. If a patient is considered to be incapacitated, or to present a threat to themselves or the public-at-large, he or she can be legally detained by the use of such reasonable force as is necessary to prevent elopement.

CONSENT FORMS

The medical record may include several different consent forms, each for a particular purpose. Every patient, or their representative, is asked to sign a consent form at the time he or she is admitted to a hospital. This covers routine procedures. Handing an individual who may be in great pain or under great stress a preprinted form that he or she is asked to quickly read and sign does not meet the legal definition of informed consent. (Many legal authorities have asserted that the form is not worth the paper it is printed on!) To meet all legal criteria, informed consent must incorporate the two primary elements described previously.

Many state statutes do not define a specific requirement for a signed consent form. If a practitioner has documented in the medical record that he or she has personally presented the patient with information that meets all of the required elements of full disclosure, that the patient understood the materials presented and has verbally assented, the practitioner's notes may serve as evidence in lieu of a signed form. A consent form may not include any language that prevents the patient from withdrawing or revoking their consent.

RESPONSIBILITY FOR OBTAINING INFORMED CONSENT

It is the legal responsibility of the *practitioner* (usually a physician) who has ordered, or who will perform, the proposed procedure or treatment to obtain that patient's informed consent. He or she is required to confirm that the information they had presented to their capacitated patient met the requirements of full disclosure. Practitioners as a general rule are not permitted to delegate this responsibility to anyone else.

Staff nurses should not be responsible for providing full disclosure or obtaining informed consent. This was considered appropriate in a case in which the court ruled that the information the nurse provided was within that particular nurse's scope of practice. These situations usually involve only advanced practice nurses such as clinical nurse specialists or nurse practitioners. However, in all instances, the information that is given to the patient must come from that professional who is most qualified by education and experience.

WITNESSES TO INFORMED CONSENT

A witness may not be required to validate informed consent. This will depend on the particular state's laws. The institution may have a specific policy regarding witnesses. In some hospitals there may be a policy that requires that a registered nurse witness a consent form. In signing as witness, the participant is attesting that the patient was competent, capacitated, that he or she signed voluntarily, and that the patient's signature is authentic—it is that of the person giving the consent. The witness does not incur any liability for failure to obtain informed consent.

ADVANCE DIRECTIVES

Related to the issues of consent are those of advance directives. There have been a number of lawsuits that have claimed that health care providers have failed to comply with an advance directive to some degree or another: Treatment had been initiated when it should not have been, or appropriate intervention was not attempted when it should have been. When this becomes an issue in a malpractice lawsuit, the paralegal and lay reviewer will be challenged to confirm the propriety of the medical treatment from their review of the medical record and the language of an advance directive.

Each state now has a statute that allows any adult to prepare some form of legal document that affirms their desires and preferences for medical care in the event that they are no longer able to do so. These documents may be referred to in terms such as "right-to-die," "natural death," or "living will." They express the concept of self-determination and recognize that every person has the inherent right to refuse any and all extraordinary life-saving measures in those situations where such efforts would only prolong suffering and/or when there is no reasonable hope of survival.

With few exceptions, each state provides a different written format for the instrument. In some states the patient is required to use that form, in others they are not. Regardless of its source, the language of the form must conform to the particular state's laws. Oral living wills are usually not legally binding. A capacitated patient's statements regarding election to refuse treatment are binding on health care providers. A documented living will, written or oral, will likely be accepted by a court as definitive evidence of a patient's wishes.

Under the Patient Self-Determination Act of 1990 (PSDA, the Act), an individual state's law will control and the format and language of any type of directive must conform to the particular state's statute. The PSDA requires hospitals to develop policies and procedures that recognize a patient's rights under various state laws to accept or refuse medical treatment.

Certain elements are common to most statutes. There is always a stipulation that the subject patient has been determined to be incompetent or incapacitated before the advance directive may be implemented. There is usually a requirement that the person be suffering from a terminal illness and that there is no likely possibility of recovery, or that he or she is in an intractable coma, persistent vegetative state, or so profoundly debilitated that they show no promise of response to treatment. Often these living wills are written in very broad terms that deal primarily with "extraordinary" medical intervention in those situations where there is "no hope." They may include such language as no "heroic" efforts, but do not address such basic life sustaining medical treatments as nutrition and hydration. These have been very contentious issues.

As a general rule, the various state statutes prescribe that any advance directive can go into effect only after a *physician* has made a determination that one or more of the above conditions are present. Some statutes require that a second physician concur in the decision.

The PSDA requires hospitals and nursing homes that receive federal funds such as from Medicare and/or Medicaid to inform each patient of his or her rights. They are also required to provide *written* information about advance directives to every patient at the time of his or her admission. There must be documentation in the medical record confirming that a patient had or had not prepared any type of advance directive. The act does not require that a copy of the document be included in the record.

The laws of each state have established procedures and directives to guarantee that advance directives will be carried out by appropriate health care professionals. The health care provider who makes every reasonable effort to carry out a directive should, as a general rule, be immune from civil or criminal liability.

Conflicts inevitably arise when family members or others who have a direct interest in the patient's welfare (or estate) do not understand the legal, medical, and ethical implications of advance directives. Physicians may be threatened with malpractice lawsuits by family members who demand compliance or, conversely, noncompliance with the provisions of a directive they personally may find difficult to accept. Many state statutes provide immunity from liability for physicians who make good-faith decisions about life-sustaining interventions initiated in certain circumstances.

There may be criminal penalties for individuals who tamper with or conceal the existence of an advance directive—no matter how well-intentioned their motives. Family members are frequently angered when emergency medical technicians or other rescue personnel initiate CPR in a victim's home in spite of being told that the victim had signed an advance directive that specifically forbids any such efforts. The victim's family must understand that, by law, emergency personnel must make every possible life-saving effort. *Only a physician can implement an advance directive.*

THE NO-CODE ORDER

Another contentious issue that occasionally arises in malpractice lawsuits is the presence or absence of a "no-code" order. This is a less formal type of advance directive, in that no prescribed legal document is required—a hospital form will usually be used—but it may require a witness to the patient's signature. In the absence of a signed and witnessed advance directive, any capacitated individual has the right to request that their physician write a "no-code" or "Do not resuscitate" (DNR) order to be implemented when a change in their medical status warrants it. If a capacitated patient has made this request, their attending physician must write this as an order in the patient's chart. All discussions with the patient or appropriate family members regarding the decision should also be documented thoroughly by the physician.

When a malpractice claim revolves around such an order, the reviewer must confirm from the medical record:

1. Was such an order given?
2. Who gave it?
3. Was the order *written*?
4. According to the medical record *when was it written*?
5. Was it prepared and carried out in a proper manner?
6. Is their any documentation indicating who requested the order?

Verbal DNR Orders

A verbal DNR order presents an unacceptable risk to medical and nursing staff. As a general rule, to protect themselves from liability, physicians or nurses should not accept and/or act on a verbal DNR order. The common approach to such an order is: "If it was not written, it was not given." In the absence of a written no-code order (or physician-activated advance directive) the appropriate staff must react as if the order simply does not exist. In the event of cardiac and/or respiratory arrest, they must initiate full-code protocols and begin all appropriate resuscitative efforts immediately—even if the patient is terminally ill. If a DNR order has been written, they should not call a code. If they do, this could expose them to charges of malpractice, battery, or possibly criminal negligence.

Failure to take what a court might consider to have been the appropriate action under the circumstances may be cause for a claim of malpractice. Defending such a claim could be very difficult without evidence of a *written* DNR order. The medical record reviewer should attempt to ascertain whether or not what may have been a verbal order conveniently appears at some point as a written order. Where and when does it appear in the record?

REFERENCE

Richards, Edward P., and Katharine Rathbun. 1983. *Medical Risk Management: Preventive Legal Strategies for Health Care Providers*. Aspen Publishers, Inc.

3

The Medical Record

DEFINITION OF A MEDICAL RECORD

The medical record, or the "health record" as it is sometimes called, is a patient-identifiable compilation of narrative or descriptive information and data that has been derived and recorded by any number or type of health care providers to document the nature and quality of care and services provided to a particular patient over a defined period of time, and to identify the individual providers of such care and services.

The medical record, in its entirety, is a written chronicle of the medical, nursing, and other types of care that a patient has received or is expected to receive. This includes medical management prior to admission to an institution, the medical and nursing regimen while in the institution, or an anticipated course of treatment after discharge.

HISTORICAL PERSPECTIVE

The techniques and procedures for setting up and maintaining medical records evolved during the late nineteenth and early twentieth centuries. Prior to that, there were various types of health care delivery systems in place. These ranged from the solo practitioner—the "country doctor" in rural or small-town settings—to independent physicians affiliated with hospitals, but not employed by them. The "specialist" was an evolving approach to medical care, as were consultants from various disciplines. A physician treated his (or her—where there were female physicians) patients in their homes or in the doctor's office and—where there was an affiliation and accessibility—in a hospital.

The patient generally had only one physician, in independent practice, who addressed most of his or her basic medical needs. This was the "family" doctor who treated a group of patients over an extended period of time, literally from cradle to grave in many instances. He or she maintained the medical records in filing cabinets in his or her office. Each file served as a personal memorandum of the patient's medical history and as a business record for billing purposes.

With the advent of specialty and subspecialty medical care, physicians began to see only a select group of patients—those whose condition or illness was the subject of the specialist's field and expertise. In many instances, this increased the number of individuals seen in physicians' individual or group practice, but reduced the frequency of their visits.

In the present health care delivery system, there is a strong likelihood that a patient will be seen by several physicians (or nurse practitioners) in clinics or in group practices that gradually absorbed many independent practices. Today, both patients and the assortment of practitioners they may encounter during follow-up visits can be virtual strangers to each other. When admitted to a hospital today, a patient might be admitted and attended to by a "hospitalist"—a new breed of hospital-based physician. This physician may be obliged to review the notes of several prior providers of care before personally encountering, assessing, and treating each patient for the first, and perhaps only, time.

Traditionally, the hospital provided various services such as surgery, obstetrics, room, and board. Nursing care was primarily attending to the patient's comfort, feeding, personal hygiene, medications, and carrying out very basic nursing procedures such as dressing changes, cast care, and monitoring vital signs. All very low tech compared to the science of nursing practice today. Nursing care was most often provided by nuns or by nursing students enrolled in the hospital's school of nursing (relatively few of which still exist). They were in residence at the hospital and were available virtually around the clock.

Then, as now, nurses documented the care they provided in the patient's chart. Such notes were typically a very basic narrative of what had been done for the patient during a particular shift, including such events as feeding, bathing, medications, and vital signs. "Nursing diagnoses" were unheard of at that time. (There are many nurses who feel that they should have remained that way!)

The medical record, particularly the nurses' notes, was merely a repository of basic information, and not the primary means of communication between an array of health care providers as it is in today's hospital setting. Essentially, there were only two providers—the physician and their "handmaidens"—the nurses, whose primary duty was to carry out the physician's orders—without question! Lawsuits against nurses were virtually unheard of. The hospital might be sued, the physician might be sued, but the nurse who merely carried out an order was considered immune. In our litigious society of today, any provider of health care is liable for a lawsuit. Malpractice lawsuits against nurses have increased markedly in the past four decades.

Physicians' entries were usually orders to be carried out and a brief summary of the patient's current status. Typically, imperious physicians did not address or even acknowledge nurses, let alone consult with them. (Those were the days when nurses were obliged to stand when a physician entered.) Other than the patient's graphic chart of vital signs, nurses' notes were deemed largely irrelevant to the physician. If the physician wished to know, he or she elected to ask. The physician did not condescend to read nurses' notes. As we shall see in a later chapter, the review and analysis of the record will require a determination of whether or not physicians read nurses' notes and conversely—and if, in fact, all members of the health care team read appropriate documentation by others. The question will be was there ongoing, effective communication?

These earlier dynamics became obsolete as medical technology developed at a rapid pace after World War II. Evolving technology and complexity of patient care demanded thorough documentation by all practitioners and providers from a variety of disciplines—medical, nursing, therapy, psychosocial, religion, and nutrition, among others. Nursing came to be recognized as a professional discipline, as a science. Nursing education began to shift from hospital based diploma programs to college and university undergraduate and graduate degree programs. As nurses acquired increasing autonomy in professional practice and were permitted to implement procedures using defined protocols and/or independent judgment, nursing roles and responsibilities evolved and expanded.

With these expanded roles and responsibilities came a concomitant risk for increased legal liability. Nursing documentation, in various formats, became a critical method of risk management strategy. The concept of the health care team was established and the need to communicate essential patient-care information among all members of the team became paramount. The medical record became the primary means of such communication in the effort of continuity of patient care, quality control, cost control, and risk management.

STANDARDS AND PURPOSES OF THE MEDICAL RECORD

The standards and purposes of medical records in hospitals or other health care facilities are largely prescribed by the Joint Commission of Accreditation of Healthcare Organizations (JCAHO). These are set forth in the *Comprehensive Accreditation Manual for Hospitals* and in its other discipline-specific accreditation manuals. Selected JCAHO standards and purposes are outlined below.

JOINT COMMISSION OF ACCREDITATION OF HEALTHCARE ORGANIZATIONS' STANDARDS AND PURPOSES OF THE MEDICAL RECORD

Standards

- The record will confirm that the patient has been properly identified, assessed, and admitted to the institution.
- The record will reflect timely and proper medical and nursing intervention and treatment based on medical diagnoses.
- Such intervention and treatment will be completely and accurately documented.
- The documentation in the medical record will conform to the standards defined by JCAHO and the U. S. Department of Health and Human Services.
- All such documentation will be retained and protected by the institution for the prescribed period of time.

Purposes

- Facilitate the best possible patient care.
- Direct and document the medical regimen.
- Direct and document the nursing process.
- Document patient care management and the patient's response to and effectiveness of medical and nursing interventions.
- Provide a central repository of data to be communicated to all members of the health care team including providers outside of the institution.
- Establish a business record for the institution that will serve as a basis for financial reimbursement.
- Establish a legal record to protect the rights and interests of the patient, the institution, and the providers of care.
- Compile information for the institution's quality assurance, risk management, and peer review functions.
- Collect data for scientific research and continuing education in relevant fields.
- Present evidence to satisfy requirements for continuing accredi-

tation and/or licensing by the JCAHO and by state and federal agencies.

Standards

The JCAHO provides detailed requirements for the maintenance of medical records by hospitals. As with hospital medical records, private office record-keeping styles evolved during a period that demanded less comprehensive record keeping than is necessary today. However, there is no comparable set of standards for the private office records of physicians. As a result, there is a wide variation in the format, content, and quality of these.

Purposes

In addition to documenting patient care, the records have also come to serve a number of other purposes. The record is a business document, but it is first and foremost a medical document, and second a legal document. As a legal document it will provide evidence of the type and quality of care that a patient received at the hands of those caregivers whose orders, progress notes, and various reports are included in it.

From the perspective of risk management, the record will be crucial in preventing or mitigating the adverse consequences of malpractice litigation. Ultimately, it may serve as the foundation for a defense in malpractice claims or lawsuits. It is often stated that "a good medical record is the best defense." It will be if it is complete, well prepared, and well organized. The overall quality of the record will be the determining factor. Although the medical record is frequently defined and focused on as a legal document, this actually is the least important aspect of its definition.

The *principal function* of the record is to facilitate *planning and continuity in patient care.* The objective is to provide consistency of interpretation and integrity of information. Nonpatient care requirements can distract providers from the three principal purposes of the record. These are:

1. Ensure continuity of care by all providers;
2. provide instant access to the most current information and data on a patient's status;
3. provide a means to audit the quality of such care.

SIGNIFICANCE OF THE MEDICAL RECORD IN LEGAL PROCEEDINGS

Medical records are critical in all medical-legal issues. They are usually admissible as evidence. They will be the starting point in the lawsuit and will carry enormous weight in all legal proceedings involving medical or nursing malpractice, personal injury from causes other than malpractice, workers' compensation, SSI disability, child custody, and product liability.

In a personal injury suit or disability claim, the record will provide evidence of the nature of the individual's injuries, the course of treatment, residual disfigurement or impairment, and the prognosis for recovery. It is the basic legal document in any malpractice litigation. Here, however, the record takes on entirely new and more complex connotations. The plaintiff has alleged that his or her injury occurred while undergoing medical treatment, or that a previous injury was exacerbated by such treatment. The significance of the contents becomes of paramount importance. Review and analysis of the documentation requires a more intense and detailed scrutiny. The focus of this book will be on the medical record in malpractice litigation.

When a patient who alleges injury caused by malpractice consults an attorney to seek his or her legal advice regarding the merits of their claim and the possibility of filing a lawsuit, the attorney will decide to accept or reject the case on its apparent merits. If the attorney accepts it, the next step is likely to be to obtain and review the patient's—now client's—medical record. Considering the investment in time and money demanded of the attorney who commits to a malpractice lawsuit on behalf of a plaintiff, or a defendant, the best record may be the one that persuades that attorney that such an investment is not warranted—that the case can not be successfully prosecuted or is simply not defensible.

The review and analysis will focus on the events surrounding the alleged incident of malpractice, but will also encompass an appraisal of the overall quality and credibility of the record. The strongest case for the plaintiff will derive from documented specific incidents of apparent negligence on the part of a nurse, physician, or other health care provider. It can also partly derive by inference from undocumented but assumed certain events. In this latter case, the plaintiff's attorney will be challenged to justify such assumptions in order to cast doubt on the credibility of all or any part of the record.

The credibility of the record will be attacked on two fronts: (1) consistency and (2) completeness. If deficiencies in either or both of these can be demonstrated to a jury, the plaintiff's claims will be supported and will likely sustain an award for damages. The plaintiff's medical record provides his or her attorney with the single most effective weapon in assaulting the defendant's credibility and competency.

The record, as the primary source of the facts and circumstances surrounding the incident at issue, will invariably be offered as evidence in the courtroom. When introduced at a trial, the content of the record is assumed to be factual. If any significant document can be shown to be missing, inaccurate, or untruthful, the credibility of the entire record may be called into question. The legal implications of tampering with a record will be discussed further in chapter 8.

The attorney for each side will examine the record to evaluate its content and its usefulness in support of his or her case. The adequacy of the record will make or break a case. If it demonstrates significant deficiencies in care (breach of duty) it will severely hinder a defense to charges of malpractice. If it is complete, accurate, and factual, it may serve to repudiate any or all allegations of negligence. A well-organized, well-written record may provide the best defense for the competent provider of health care. A disorganized, sloppily written collection of documents may evince indefensible incompetency.

It may not, in and of itself, prove the degree of breach in the standards of care required for malpractice, but it certainly will attest to substandard care of some degree. The court will attempt to give a physician or nurse defendant the benefit of the doubt in those cases where blame is difficult to assign or events or circumstances are unclear or ambiguous. But this attempt will not extend to ambiguities or uncertainties presented by incompetency in documentation.

If the documentation contained in the record is FACT (Factual, Accurate, Complete, Timely) that is, if the record is tight, the plaintiff's case may not be. As many as one out of four malpractice suits are decided from the patient/plaintiff's medical record. Much of what a reviewer will do will be the preparation of an accurate, concise chronology of events described in the record and presentation of these in a concise, meaningful summary report. The various facts, data, and questions derived from the review and analysis of the medical record may also be used by an attorney in drafting or answering interrogatories, in the preparation for depositions, and eventually at a trial.

> Ironically, the focus on the medical record as a legal document has reduced both its legal and its medical effectiveness. Medical personnel, constantly told that "the good medical record is the best defense" miss the point that the good medical record is valuable only to the extent that it documents the actual rendering of good medical care. A medical record can be legally disastrous if it demonstrates the incompetence of the underlying medical care. Poor documentation is actually an advantage to an incompetent defendant whose best defense is obfuscation. A poor record may prevent the medical care providers from establishing the good care they gave the patient, but a good record is not a substitute for good care.
>
> The confusion between good medical records and good medical care has helped destroy the usefulness of medical records. Many

records administrators believe that the more information in the record, the better the record is. Even if this excess information is accurate and well organized, it dilutes the medically necessary information. Physicians and nurses will have difficulty finding medically necessary information in a timely manner. This leads to substandard medical care and potential malpractice litigation. Bigger medical records are not better medical records. (Richards and Rathbun 1993, 186)

Legal Criteria for Use of the Medical Record as Evidence in Litigation

In order for a medical record to be introduced as evidence in litigation, the following legal criteria must be met:

1. The record being presented to the court is, in fact that of the individual named as a party in the lawsuit—the patient, the plaintiff.
2. The various documents contained in the record were prepared concurrent with the events described in them, or as close to those times as possible.
3. The record was prepared and maintained in accordance with all statutory requirements and in accordance with the policies and procedures of the institution.
4. The record was prepared by persons who had direct knowledge of those events described in it.
5. The record was created during the regular course of business.
6. The record was prepared and complete before litigation was initiated.
7. The documents contained in the record, either original or duplicate are, as far as possible, of a quality as to be readable and identifiable as to content and source.
8. The record was obtained legally. (Adapted from Appleby and Tarver 1994, 138)

THE HEARSAY RULE AND MEDICAL RECORDS

The admissibility of the medical record as evidence is governed by the "Hearsay Rule." The rule affirms that one individual can not testify as to the truth of what another individual has stated. A witness can testify only as to what was said, not to the truth or accuracy of the statement.

This rule arises from the need of opposing counsel to cross-examine each witness and examine each document to determine truthfulness.

The legal basis for the rule is that, if a statement made out of court is to be accepted as evidence, the person who was merely witness to the statement—which they now repeat in court—can not be questioned about the truthfulness of the statement. The court will demand that the person who actually made the statement be brought into the courtroom, sworn in, and asked to repeat the statement, and attest under oath to its accuracy and truthfulness.

If the hearsay rule were applied to a medical record, each person who made an entry in the record would have to be brought into the courtroom, sworn in, and asked to identify every entry they made, and explain and justify each one. Because of the nightmarish logistical and time-consuming problems this would create, the courts have made an exception to the rule for medical records. Such documents may be admitted into evidence without the requirement that each and every individual who made an entry be available in court for cross-examination. If the originator's physical presence is required, he or she can be called as a witness to the facts.

Requirements of the Hearsay Rule

The exception of the hearsay rule for medical records requires that the record meet five basic requirements:

1. The record was compiled in the "regular course of business"; it is truly a business record and all entries pertain to the provision of medical or nursing care only.
2. Each entry was made by an individual who had personal knowledge of the event or information in the entry, or that the information was received directly from someone who had such personal knowledge.
3. The individual who made the entry was authorized to do so.
4. Each entry was made at a time concurrent with the condition or event described, or as soon as possible thereafter—a "reasonable delay."
5. That the medical record was prepared and maintained according to all applicable protocols, procedures, laws, rules, and regulations.

REFERENCES

Appleby, Kristyn S., and Joanne Tarver. 1994. *Medical Records Review.* 2d ed. John Wiley & Sons, Inc.

Joint Commission on Accreditation of Healthcare Organizations. 1997. *Comprehensive Accreditation Manual for Hospitals.*

Richards, Edward P., and Katharine Rathbun. 1993. *Law and the Physician: A Practical Guide.* Little, Brown and Co.

4

The Medical Record: Ownership, Access, and Retention

OWNERSHIP OF THE MEDICAL RECORD

The question of ownership of a medical record and the rights involved is addressed from the perspectives of the provider of health care and of the patient.

> In the information age, it is increasingly difficult to determine who controls or should control health information and who should control the value of the information that is shared or integrated. The issue of information ownership in the healthcare industry is even more complex because of special privacy and security laws and regulations that apply to the often sensitive information involved, based on traditional concerns for patient confidentiality. Another trend in health information law—that of stronger protection of patients' rights to access their medical information—further complicates the analysis of who owns health information. When the question "Who owns health information?" is asked, the real meaning of the question may be any of the following:
>
> 1. Who may access data?
> 2. Who may mine or manipulate data?
> 3. Who may use data and for what purpose?
> 4. Who may sell data?
> 5. Who may disclose or publish data?
> 6. Who must pay to access, use, publish or sell data?

7. Who is required to disclose data in response to subpoenas or court orders? (Waller and Alcantara 1998, 28)

The Ownership Rights of the Provider

It has been traditionally held that the hospital or physician that generates and maintains a record is the "owner" of it. This proprietary right confers not only the right of possession, but also the right to determine who may have access to the record and for what purposes. It is also generally held that the provider's "ownership" is subject to the patient's rights regarding the information contained in his or her record. The institution maintains legal ownership of a patient's medical record, and physicians own patient records that are maintained in their offices. In each setting, these are business records that are necessary to the proper administration of the institution or conduct of a practice. With ownership comes the responsibility for proper maintenance and protection of the records from loss, destruction, or alteration.

The American Medical Association (AMA) considers the content of the record to be the property of the physician. The AMA has stated that: "[N]otes made in treating a patient are primarily for the physician's own use and constitute his personal property.... [O]n request of the patient a physician should provide a copy or a summary of the record to the patient... an attorney or other person designated by the patient" (AMA 1992, 32).

Although the institution or physician has control over the physical record, the question of ownership of the information contained in it has become increasingly problematical in today's information age. "Even under the traditional rule, however, no one person or entity can be truly said to 'own' patient-identifiable information... if what is meant by ownership is the ability to exercise complete sovereignty over the information—to disclose, sell, destroy, alter, or determine who shall access to it at will" (Waller and Alcantara 1998, 29).

Continuing developments in computerized medical records have begun to generate a myriad of new issues of ownership. As patient records from different providers and institutions are integrated, questions of proprietary rights, dissemination, accessibility, alterability, corruptibility, and confidentiality are being raised. At this time, there are relatively few legal precedents that address such issues. The sharing and marketing of patient-identifiable information has created a plethora of questions and issues regarding privacy versus profit and research versus exploitation. These matters are beyond the scope of this book.

The Ownership Rights of the Patient

Providers may, by convention, own a record, but this does not, as noted previously, confer unqualified power and absolute right. Their proprietary rights and responsibilities are imposed by various federal and state laws. Most states recognize the ownership rights of patients: (1) to have access to the information contained in their medical record (with certain exceptions), (2) to make copies of it, (3) to make corrections or insert addenda, and (4) to the preservation of its confidentiality. However, state statutes typically do not address the patient's right of ownership of the record itself, but rather the information contained in it.

"The plain fact is that patients have a proprietary interest in their own medical records. At the very least the *information* contained in medical records is the property of the patient. But for the patient, the information would not exist! To require the assistance of counsel to get such records unfairly and unnecessarily burdens a patient who is trying to obtain what is rightfully his" (Wecht 1978, 9). The patient's right of ownership is the right to control the publication and dissemination of the information assembled about him or her.

ACCESS TO THE MEDICAL RECORD

The collected documents—in whatever format—are the property of the institution or physician. The collected data belongs to the patient. The right of physical possession—of ownership—is not absolute. It does not mean that access to the content of the record can be completely denied to anyone outside of the facility. As a general rule, under common law, a patient has the right to review the content of his or her record and submit appropriate additions and corrections for inclusion. He or she may not alter or remove any document that is already part of their record.

In 1977, the Privacy Protection Study Commission, which had been created under the 1974 Federal Privacy Act, prepared a report that defined a number of recommendations regarding the rights of patients to access their medical records. The 1974 act is discussed further in chapter 6. In the report, the commission recommended that both federal and state statutes be implemented or adapted to provide an individual who is the subject of a medical record maintained by a health care provider the right to access the record, including the right to read and copy its contents (Privacy Protection Study Commission 1977, 298).

At the time of this writing, one half of the states have laws in effect which grant patients access to their medical records in the possession of hospitals or physicians. The laws vary considerably by state (Johnson and Wolfe 1995, 35, 39; also see appendix II). Most define the criteria and procedures for access. Even those states that grant access may impose a variety of restrictive limitations. For example:

- The statute may apply different requirements for hospitals, mental health institutions, or physicians.
- Access may be granted to the patient only and/or the patient's attorney or other legal representative.
- The statute may permit only an examination and review of the record or also the right to have a copy of it.
- Access may be permitted to the entire record or only a summary of it.
- The custodian may have discretion to release the record.
- Physicians may retain the right to withhold or release a record.
- Certain predefined conditions may be required such as demonstrated relevancy to litigation. A court order may be required. "Good cause" may have to be shown.

Various state statutes may include specific disclosure laws that allow access without the consent or the knowledge of the patient. An adult can authorize access to his or her medical record by an attorney, a third party payer, or any other legal representative on his or her behalf. If an individual lacks the legal capacity to sign an authorization, his or her spouse, children, parents, or their legal guardian may be legally authorized to do so. A subpoena will generally open any record, and an individual can request a subpoena to gain access to the records.

A number of state statutes permit direct access; a patient does not have to initiate a formal legal procedure to obtain his or her records. Once a claim has been properly filed for workman's compensation, statutes usually allow access to relevant records. In some jurisdictions, there may be a requirement that only the patient's attorney can initiate such a request. The procedure and requirements can be quite involved. Custodians attempt to discourage frivolous inquiries. There is a mistaken belief that providing patients access to their medical record will give them an incentive to a file a lawsuit. There is no evidence to support this belief.

A patient, family member, or third party may request an opportunity to review the original medical record. This may be done while the patient is still in the hospital or at any time after discharge. For other than the patient, a properly executed authorization form will required. There is usually a request format or document required of the patient themselves. To preserve the integrity of the record, the institution may reserve the right to define the time, the place, the participants, and the supervision of the examination of the original file.

Some state statutes may require that copies of a patient's record can not be released until it is complete. They may define a period of time within which this must be accomplished. This may be up to a number of weeks after the patient's discharge, or demise—if this had occurred during his or her hospital stay.

In those instances where the patient is permitted to have a copy of his or her record, the custodian should provide it for a reasonable processing and copying fee. There have been numerous incidents of institutions charging unreasonably high fees to provide copies of medical records to patients and attorneys involved in cases of malpractice. A number of states have now outlawed these excesses by specifying a maximum per-page charge. The statutory limitations on such fees should be confirmed and compared to those required by the custodian of the record.

Statutory Restrictions on Release

Certain documents contained in a medical record may not, by law, be released without proper authority. These usually include records relating to psychiatric diagnoses and treatment, which contain information that would be considered privileged and confidential. Twenty-seven states and the District of Columbia do permit patients direct access to their mental health records (Johnson and Wolfe 1995, 39; also see appendix II).

The Federal Drug Abuse and Treatment Act of 1972 (21 USC § 1175) requires that any patient records pertaining to treatment for substance abuse are not to be released without a court order. That determination will be made only after the court weighs the risk of harm to the patient against any possible benefit to be derived. These restrictions are discussed further in chapter 6.

Accessibility by Health Care Providers and Others

During the time that a patient is in the hospital, his or her medical record is available to any member of the health care team involved in the care of that patient. Student nurses and nursing faculty are permitted to review patients' charts to prepare for and carry out clinical assignments—the patients' consent is usually not required or requested. If a person is readmitted to the institution, all of his or her prior medical records on file will be requested and sent to the admitting unit.

During a hospital stay and for a defined period of time after discharge, the patient's medical record will continue to be reviewed. Quality assurance and risk management staff routinely review charts as part of their administrative functions. Representatives of insurance companies will review the charts of patients whom they insure. Various governmental agencies and programs such as Medicare or Medicaid also have access for auditing purposes. Records also provide data for scientific research in medicine, nursing, and several other disciplines. There are usually very strict guidelines and protocols applying to access by researchers. Requests by outside individuals or agencies are routinely submitted to an internal review panel for evaluation of the proposed research and a determination that patient-subject confidentiality will be guaranteed. The patient-subject may or may not be made aware of the research involving their records.

STATUTORY REQUIREMENTS FOR RECORD KEEPING

Various federal and state laws and regulations govern the retention and release of medical records.

Federal Laws and Regulations

Medicare "Conditions of Participation" for hospitals, home health agencies, states, long-term care facilities, specialized providers, and suppliers require varying time periods according to each entity or unless state laws prescribe longer periods (42 Code of Federal Regulations [CFR], 482.24 et *sequitar*). As a general rule, Medicare and Medicaid records must be available for review and for verification of charges for a five-year period. The Conditions of Participation for hospices, ambulatory surgical services, and HMOs do not specify a retention period.

The Labor and Industries Occupational Safety and Health Administration (OSHA) requires that employee medical records be retained for the period of employment plus thirty years, except in cases where the employee worked less than one year, if these records are provided to the employee upon the termination of employment. OSHA also requires that employee exposure records be preserved and maintained for at least thirty years.

State Laws and Regulations

It is generally advised that in the absence of specific state requirements for record retention, health care entities—physicians and institutions—should retain medical records for at least the period specified by a state's statute of limitations. In reviewing a medical record, one should be aware of the discovery rule as it affects the statute of limitations, and, if the patient was a minor at the time of the alleged injury, appropriate state laws regarding minors and statutes of limitations. In accordance with the various state laws, an adult usually has from one to four years after the occurrence of an injury to file a claim for medical malpractice. In the case of a minor, the statute is usually extended until the patient reaches majority, and for a prescribed period thereafter as defined by the state law.

The reviewer should be cognizant of issues that may arise with statutes of limitation in that many states define the limitation period differently. As previously discussed, the statute of limitations may begin to run: (1) on the date when the alleged malpractice actually occurred—whether the patient was aware of it or not; (2) on the date when the patient was last treated by the physician for the illness or condition that is the focus of the allegation; or (3) on the date the patient discovered, or should have discovered, that he or she was a possible victim of malpractice. In those jurisdictions in which the statute of limitations begins to run from the date of discovery, it is possible that a malpractice suit could be filed at an indefinite time after the patient was last treated.

RETENTION OF MEDICAL RECORDS

The American Medical Association and the American Medical Record Association recommend, as a general rule, that the medical records of patients who had been treated in an acute care setting be retained for at least a ten year period. The JCAHO accreditation standards recommend a period of retention according to anticipated future need of a record in continuing patient care; or for other purposes such as medical and/or nursing research, education, or as required by federal or state laws and regulations. A hospital or any other health care entity may elect to retain patient records indefinitely depending on the availability of storage facilities and ongoing maintenance costs.

It is the responsibility of a facility's medical records department to develop retention schedules that comply with an array of legal, regulatory, and accreditation requirements and that meet the needs of patients, practitioners, researchers, and other users with a legitimate right to access. The custodian of the records is responsible for developing guidelines that specify those documents to be retained, for how long, and in what format—paper, microfilm, or computer disk.

Retention of Medical Records by Physicians

It is recommended that physicians' offices have a formal, written records retention policy that provides for convenient, economical storage for the periods prescribed by law and/or regulations, and that provide reasonably quick access. The statutory requirements on how long a physician must retain private office records vary in number and by state.

From a legal aspect, the statute of limitations for medical malpractice in the state where the physician maintains his or her practice would be considered the absolute minimum period that patient records should be maintained.

As in any health care facility, from a risk management point of view, it is desirable for all physician's records to be retained indefinitely. Realistically, for a physician's office this may be physically impossible and financially unfeasible. The amount of space required could cause potential confusion and impede access to currently active records. (A college in Allentown, Pennsylvania, stores students' infirmary records accumulated over decades in a room under the gilded dome and behind the clock faces in the tower of "Old Main.")

An "active" record is considered to be that of any patient who has been treated within a preceding two-year period, unless that patient has died. If a patient has not been seen by a physician within such time period, and does not have a continuing medical condition, the physician may elect to assign that patient's file to inactive status and arrange to store it accordingly—perhaps at a distant commercially operated site. A summary of each of these records is usually retained in a file or on a computer disk in the event that the patient is seen again or an emergency situation arises. Reference to the summary will expedite care in either the physician's office or in a hospital until the complete record can be retrieved.

Retention Recommendations of the American Health Information Management Association

Unless longer periods of time are required by state or federal law, the American Health Information Management Association (AHIMA) recommends that patient health information be retained for the following minimum time periods.

- Patient health records (adults): ten years after the most recent encounter
- Patient health records (minors): age of majority plus statute of limitations
- Diagnostic images (e.g., x-ray films): five years
- Disease index: ten years
- Fetal heart monitoring records: ten years after the infant reaches the age of majority
- Master patient index: permanently
- Operative index: ten years

- Physician index: ten years
- Registration of birth: permanently
- Registration of death: permanently
- Register of surgical procedures: permanently (AHIMA, *Journal of the American Health Information Management Association*, January 1997)

DESTRUCTION OF MEDICAL RECORDS

As a general rule, medical records may be destroyed only under certain, limited circumstances. The demise of the subject-patient is an accepted one. After a reasonable period of time has elapsed after the individual's death, his or her record might be destroyed. The statute of limitations for medical malpractice in the state of jurisdiction is the norm. It has been recommended that the family of a deceased patient be advised of the impending action and given an opportunity to obtain a copy of the record before it is destroyed. The rationale is not to provide substantive evidence for possible legal action, but because it could provide invaluable information for other family members regarding genetic diseases and traits and their implications for survivors. There appears to be no data available on the extent to which this recommendation is followed by physicians or other health care entities.

When a physician sells his or her practice or consolidates it with another, patient records routinely transfer. If a physician retires from practice, dies, or is barred from practice and his or her office records are not transferred to another physician, these may be destroyed at a reasonable time after the physician ceases to practice. Medical ethics demand that every effort should be made in an attempt to contact all patients before destroying the records. Each should be advised of the practitioner's circumstances and advised of the right to claim, or transfer, a file within a reasonable time. When that defined time has elapsed, any unclaimed inactive records can be destroyed. The active records of patients should be maintained by an alternate custodian, if at all possible. Arrangements might be made to have these records transferred to another physician or to a hospital. An executor may make such arrangements, or perhaps a court order may be required. Maintaining privacy of the files is essential.

REFERENCES

American Medical Association, Council on Ethical and Judicial Affairs. 1992. *Code of Medical Ethics: Current Opinions.*

Johnson, Diann, and Sidney M. Wolfe. 1995. *Medical Records: Getting Yours.* Public Citizen's Health Research Group.

Journal of the American Health Information Management Association. 1997. Issue: Retention of health information. Practice Brief. No author. Not paginated.

Privacy Protection Study Commission. 1977. *Record-keeping in the Medical-care Relationship: Personal Privacy in an Information Society*. U.S. Government Printing Office.

Waller, Adele A., and Oscar L. Alcantara. 1998. Ownership of health information in the information age. *Journal of the American Health Information Management Association* 69 (3): 28–34.

Wecht, C. H. 1978. Patient access to medical records: Yea or nay? *Legal Aspects of Medical Practice*. October 9.

5

Obtaining a Medical Record

THE FORMAL PROCESS

The formal process of obtaining a medical record is initiated after litigation has actually begun, that is, with the filing of the complaint. In the formal procedure, the means of obtaining medical records is the subpoena process. As necessary, an attorney will request a court to issue a subpoena in the course of a lawsuit. Federal Rule of Civil Procedure 34 provides that a *supoena duces tecum* may be issued to the custodian of such records. State laws and rules generally are in conformance with federal provisions. In most states, a subpoena is sufficient authority to require production of a medical record. A deposition and trial subpoena does not require a patient's prior authorization for release of his or her record.

The defendant's attorney, having no patient/plaintiff authorization for disclosure, can get the records only by court order or subpoena. He or she will move to obtain all relevant records as soon as the plaintiff's providers are identified (through deposition or interrogatories). They will immediately review these to evaluate the merits of the plaintiff's case, define their strategy, and identify all other potential defendants.

THE INFORMAL PROCESS

This is initiated before a lawsuit is filed. "At any time prior to the initiation of a lawsuit, records can be obtained through a release or authorization that has been signed by the patient or a legal representative. A patient's authorization essentially gives permission to allow copies of any personal medical records or other information . . . to be released to a designated individual or group. The term 'authorization' can be used interchangeably with 'release' or 'consent.'" (Appleby and Tarver 1994, 156).

For purposes other than requirements for patient care, information considered to be confidential can be disclosed only upon written authorization by the patient or their legal representative, or where such disclosure is authorized (or required) by federal or state law, subpoena, or court order. Many institutions use their own release form—particularly when the records are considered privileged. Examples of these would be with mental health records or treatment for substance abuse.

Special authorization forms and very strict requirements and procedures are involved in releasing records of substance abuse treatment. As discussed in chapter 6, disclosure of any information relating to substance abuse is governed by specific federal statutes codified in 42 CFR, Ch. 1, Part 2 (1983). The requirements for release pursuant to the consent of a patient's drug or alcohol abuse records are defined under 42 CFR Section 2.31.

Under the various privacy laws, an authorization for disclosure must be in proper format and signed by the patient. It is the instrument by which the person assigns the authority to a legal representative to act on his or her behalf and grants the custodian of the patient's record the authority to disclose the content of it to a third party. If the patient has died, the release form must be signed by the executor or administrator of the decedent's estate. A suggested format for an authorization form is shown below.

FORMAT FOR AN AUTHORIZATION FORM

- The exact name of the person—the patient—who is the subject of the medical records
- The specific name or general designation of the custodian (facility or person) who is directed to make the disclosure
- The exact names of the parties involved, including provider(s), patient, or other entity to whom disclosure is to be made
- A statement of valid reasons for the disclosure request
- The nature of the information that is to be disclosed
- Extent of the disclosure
- The date on which the consent for release was signed
- The date upon which the consent expires or those events, conditions, or circumstances which would void it

- An affirmation that the consent is subject to revocation at any time
- The signature of the subject of the records or their legal representative

A General Authorization/Patient Consent Form appears in 42 CFR Section 2.31(a).

Previously Signed Authorization Forms in the Medical Record

The health care institution or other provider already has the record in their possession, and usually included in the documents is a standard limited release form that had been signed previously by the patient. At some point during admission, hospitalization, or prior to treatment, the patient had likely signed a general consent form, that included permission for the health care provider not only to treat them, but also to allow access to the patient's record by any and all authorized parties, within and outside of the institution. This would include all appropriate professional staff, HMOs, health insurance companies, Blue Cross/Blue Shield, and Medicare/Medicaid.

REQUEST LETTER FORMAT

Since requests for medical records are virtually always initiated by an attorney, we will focus here on the role of the paralegal in preparing and following through on the request. In either the informal or formal process of obtaining a medical record of a plaintiff-client, the paralegal may be directed to prepare certain documents, route them, and confirm timely compliance with the request or court order. He or she must be aware of the legal procedures involved. As a general rule, a paralegal should not send a signed authorization for release of medical records to a custodian of the records without a formal letter of request signed by an attorney. A suggested format for the request letter accompanying the signed authorization for release is shown in the inset. (This format may also be used by a patient or their representative in making a request personally.)

REQUEST LETTER FORMAT

- The full, legal, name of the patient—the name under which treatment was received and which should appear on the record

- The address of the patient at the time of his or her hospitalization and treatment
- The patient's current address
- The patient's date of birth
- The Social Security number
- Any other identifying numbers, for example, insurance, HMO
- Patient's institution identification number, if known
- Inclusive dates of hospitalization and treatment
- Any other legal documents as may be required by the patient's status

IDENTIFYING THE RECORDS REQUESTED

The letter should also include a statement which, as far as possible, lists the specific records and documents being requested. Most standard authorization formats include phrases such as "any and all records" that may pertain to the circumstances surrounding the alleged incident on specified dates. In requesting a physician's narrative report, or any other records, avoid a generalized form letter. This might yield a generalized response or incomplete, useless information. Be as specific as possible, based on details in medical records and the injury or complaint identified by the patient/plaintiff. Before preparing and sending a letter, confirm these details with the client.

A narrative medical report prepared by each of the patient's treating physicians is a possible source of additional relevant information. Obtaining these can be very expensive and may contain a great deal of unneeded information and data. It is recommended that the clinical records be obtained first. After a review of these, consideration can be given to obtaining a physician's narrative report to determine if any specific information was not included or not detailed in the clinical records. It may be more cost-effective to simply request, and pay for, a complete copy of the physician's records, and develop a narrative report from them—if the physician will cooperate.

The following records are not usually requested. However they may contain important information. A subpoena may be needed to obtain these.

- Incident reports (if discoverable)
- Certain internal departmental records—(e.g., radiology, PT, OT)
- Committee minutes and reports that may have specifically addressed the incident or injury at issue

- Peer review committee reports—licensing, accreditation
- Statistical reports—patient data on mortality, infection, incidence
- Staff or other employee personnel files

Autopsy Report

In the event a patient has died, an autopsy report should be obtained. This is *essential* in a possible claim for malpractice or wrongful death. This will detail the findings of a medical examiner or coroner regarding the exact cause of death. The autopsy report may be obtained from the medical examiner or coroner using the forms and procedures they might require. It may or may not be in the medical record.

Records of Past Medical History

Determining which specific records or documents to obtain can be problematic. For either side in the case, the extent of their selection may be defined by financial considerations. Each may wish to limit their expenses by obtaining only those records that have the most relevancy to the alleged incident. If any records of the plaintiff's past medical history are not obtained initially, the attorney may have no choice but to rely on his or her client's memory. This can be a risky act of faith that could place the attorney at a distinct disadvantage in preparing the case.

It is advisable that the both the attorney and the paralegal be fully and accurately informed of their client's prior medical history. They must identify all preexisting conditions, if any, to evaluate their possible impact on the client's present status, the claims, and the merits of the case. Clients are often unaware that aggravation of a preexisting condition may actually increase the value of their case; therefore, it is imperative that their attorney have all such information.

There is also the possibility that a preexisting condition may negate the validity of the plaintiff's injuries. His or her attorney must be aware of anything the defendant's insurance carrier or counsel may learn and that could be detrimental. There must be *no surprises*! Not obtaining the records of the client's past medical history may be cost effective in the short run, but it could prove very costly in the long run—in terms of money and advantage. As a general rule, the plaintiff's attorney should obtain as complete a set as possible before filing the lawsuit.

TIMING OF THE REQUEST

It is advisable to initiate any action to obtain the medical records far enough in advance of need. The attorney or paralegal should not wait until the last minute. In requesting a subpoena, the attorney must permit the custodian sufficient time to retrieve, reproduce, and deliver the documents. The record may not be immediately available. Depending on the custodian, reproduction and delivery time can be as long as one to two months—or even longer. There have been malpractice lawsuits based on inordinate delays on the part of an attorney that had an adverse affect on a plaintiff's case.

The signed authorization must be current. In some jurisdictions it must be signed within sixty days prior to the date of the request. If the authorization form is not in compliance, it may have to be reexecuted. The client may be asked to sign a number of undated authorization forms. These can be kept on file so that records can be obtained at any time without the need to inconvenience the client each time a form may be required.

EXPENSES INVOLVED IN OBTAINING RECORDS

Before attempting to obtain a record, you should telephone or visit the medical records department of the institution and request a copy of their release guidelines, including their requirements for the format of the disclosure form, their copying procedures, timetable for delivery, and fees. The copying fee for medical records is usually based on per-page charge. In many institutions, it is done by outside copy service contractors. In many jurisdictions, medical records departments are not required to copy and/or deliver records until the copying and delivery fees are paid in advance. The maximum per-page charge may be fixed by state law.

THE CUSTODIAN'S RESPONSE TO A REQUEST FOR A MEDICAL RECORD

When the medical records department of a hospital receives a letter (or a subpoena) requesting the records of a patient, this is usually a red flag. The first sign of potential lawsuit may be a request for a copy of a present or former patient's medical record. The risk management department and the institution's counsel is alerted to the request and the possibility of a lawsuit. The attorney representing the institution will call for a medical record at the first hint of a lawsuit. The original record is usually secured to eliminate the possibility of tampering or alterations of any kind. A copy will be prepared and forwarded to the individual making the request.

The request may set in motion a review of the record by quality assurance, risk management, and counsel to predetermine the likely cause of a claim of negligence and pre-evaluate the merits of any potential claim. A quality assurance peer review of the records may be initiated. The purpose is to measure conduct in the event against the "reasonable professional standard," which any effective and successful defense will require. The reasonable professional standard may not necessarily be the same as the high quality, optimal standard defined by the institution.

An effort will be made to define the degree of exposure to liability, the possible damages to be claimed, and the strengths and weakness of their position. Contingent on the findings of the review, strategies for a possible defense in an anticipated lawsuit may be defined and implemented. Terms of a settlement proposal may be formulated.

REFERENCE

Appleby, Kristyn S., and Joanne Tarver. 1994. *Medical Records Review*. 2d ed. John Wiley & Sons, Inc.

6

Confidentiality and Privacy Issues

CONFIDENTIALITY AND PRIVACY

Over the past twenty-five years, issues of medical record confidentiality have increased significantly. With this increase comes a concurrent need for proper handling of such records by a reviewer. For reasons of professional ethics and legal liability, a medical record must be obtained, reviewed, and analyzed so as to assure patient confidentiality, privilege, and absolute privacy. (The terms "confidential" and "privileged" are used interchangeably.) Often an individual will be unaware that his or her medical records have been subpoenaed in litigation and that these records may include certain facts that are highly confidential and irrelevant to the issues of the case.

Medical records may contain extremely personal and highly sensitive information. In addition to details about an individual's physical and mental health, the records may also contain revelations about family history, sexual preferences, substance abuse, and criminal history. The data in a medical record could affect the subject's credit, employment, admission to educational institutions, and eligibility for life or health insurance and the coverage rates that will be assigned. Most insurance policy applications contain an authorization clause allowing release of information to an insurance company and a notice that a report will be filed with the Medical Information Bureau (MIB), an insurance industry–supported organization set up to detect fraudulent applications. The MIB is discussed in a later section of this chapter.

In the health care environment of today, an insurance company, employer, researcher, health maintenance organization, government agency, and a variety of hospital staff have far more access to an individual's medical record than the individual him-or herself. As previously discussed, only about one-half of the states now permit an individual access to his or her own records. It is generally very difficult for an individual to obtain a copy of his or her own record or to correct any information in that record.

Confidentiality of medical records was seriously compromised (if not sacrificed entirely) when employee health insurance plans were implemented. The employee's signature on a release form for reimbursement effectively permits full access to that employee's medical record by any number of individuals inside and outside the place of employment.

In the climate of managed care, vast databases have been assembled by health maintenance organizations, hospital ownership and management firms, insurance companies, and pharmaceutical firms. These data are being shared, sold, and otherwise widely disseminated across state lines in the absence of adequate laws, rules, and regulations—federal or state. The dissemination of medical records via fax or the Internet, their accessibility to prying eyes, their susceptibility to copying, and the legal and ethical implications of such ominous developments for confidentiality and personal privacy is beyond the scope of this book.

The right to confidentiality is not absolute, however. There have been a number of court decisions that have affirmed that any and all material that is subject to such protection must be produced or disclosed upon a showing of proper cause. Statutes dealing with confidentiality vary by state. These statutes generally require that medical records can not be disclosed to third parties without the consent of the individual who is the subject of the records. However, in most states, the records can be released without such consent in response to a subpoena.

WAIVER OF CONFIDENTIALITY

An individual's waiver of confidentiality of medical records may be either expressed or implied.

Expressed Waiver

The individual may expressly waive privilege by formal execution of a signed authorization or consent for release of his or her medical record. Any such release form should be prepared by an attorney to protect the legal rights of both the patient and the custodian of the records.

Implied Waiver

When a person initiates a malpractice or personal injury lawsuit, they effectively introduce their mental and/or physical condition as an issue in the litigation. Consequently physician-patient privilege is effectively waived, and the way is cleared for the disclosure of the medical record by means of a subpoena or a court order.

However, this waiver of privilege is not automatically established with the filing of a complaint—or an answer. The plaintiff (or the defendant, if their physical or mental condition has been offered in defense of an action) must raise the issue and assert that his or her injury or physical or mental condition was the result of the claimed incident of malpractice or other cause of personal injury.

Pennsylvania courts have held that: "the privilege of confidentiality in medical records 'evaporates' when the patient brings a personal injury action which calls into question his physical or mental condition" [in as much as the action is considered to constitute a waiver of any such privilege] [O'Boyle v. Jensen, 150 FRD 519–522. (M.D. Pa. 1993)]. Pennsylvania's rules provide no "good cause" exception for the release of records without a patient's consent.

CONFIDENTIALITY IN THE HEALTH CARE PROVIDER–PATIENT RELATIONSHIP

The Hippocratic Oath states: "Whatsoever things I see or hear concerning the life of men in attendance on the sick or even apart therefrom, which ought not to be noised abroad, I will keep silent thereon, counting such things to be as sacred secrets." The professional ethic of privilege is the essence of the physician-patient relationship as it is in the attorney-client relationship.

> Generally speaking, these statutes provide that an evidentiary privilege may be asserted on behalf of the patient with regard to physician-patient communications in judicial and quasi-judicial proceedings. In some jurisdictions this privilege has been extended to communications between a patient and nurse, psychologist, psychotherapist, or social worker. . . . In states without a privilege statute, some courts have recognized a duty on the part of a physician to remain silent. The duty has variously been interpreted to derive from an implied contract of confidentiality, a patient's constitutional right to privacy, state licensing statutes, and as a matter of public policy. (Appleby and Tarver 1994, 114)

The American Medical Association affirmed the concept of confidentiality in the *Principles of Medical Ethics* (Article 5.05), which states: "The information disclosed to a physician during the course of the relationship between physician and patient is confidential to the greatest possible degree. . . . [T]he obligation to safeguard patient confidences is subject to certain exceptions which are ethically and legally justified because of overriding social considerations."

State Laws

The privilege doctrine is guaranteed by law. Over two-thirds of the states have statutorily recognized physician-patient privilege. (For a recent listing, see Appleby and Tarver 1994, Table 4–1, 115.) These statutes define those relationships protected by the doctrine; their confidentiality provisions often parallel federal provisions. State courts have been vigorous in protecting a patient's right to have all information that has been revealed to a physician, psychiatrist, psychotherapist, and certain other health care providers kept confidential. All individuals considered to have such a relationship—physician/patient, attorney/client, priest/penitent—can not be coerced to divulge such communications. Before this can be done, the individual who has confided in the physician, attorney, or clergy must agree. The objective of the privilege doctrine is to encourage a patient to confide even the most secret matters if such would be essential to a diagnosis and plan of treatment. The legal doctrine of "qualified privilege" is shown below.

THE LEGAL DOCTRINE OF QUALIFIED PRIVILEGE

The legal doctrine of qualified privilege can be invoked in cases involving the release of otherwise confidential information. It involves statements made concerning matters regarding which one person has an interest or duty to communicate to another person with the same interests or duty. It is a conditional right of immunity that can be used as a defense to a *prima faciae* case of defamation when it can be shown that there was no malicious intent on the part of the defendant. That is, the statements were made in duty or good faith, in a reasonable manner, for a valid reason, and directed to another person with a lawful, legitimate right or need to know.

There is always a possibility that a person's medical record could include information or data that is inaccurate and that, if revealed, could defame that person. Release of any information regarding a patient's medical condition or record must be made in compliance with applicable federal and state laws. If a specific law addresses the release of such information, the qualified privilege doctrine will not offer protection if the disclosure violates that law.

Exceptions to Health Care Provider–Patient Privilege

There are a number of exceptions to the doctrine of practitioner-patient privilege and to the general principle of an individual's right to privacy. These can be very significant in the legal process.

Disclosures Made Outside the Physician-Patient Relationship

These would include information that the physician, or any other health care provider, might derive in other than a diagnosis and treatment situation. A typical example would be a physician designated by the court to examine and evaluate a party in a lawsuit or a physician who might be retained by defense counsel to conduct an independent medical examination (IME) of a plaintiff in an action or in an alternative dispute resolution situation.

A physician acting in these capacities carries out the examination of the subject for the purpose of preparing a case for a trial, hearing, or other legal proceeding. He or she may or may not be called as an expert medical witness. His or her role is primarily that of examiner and evaluator. In this capacity a predetermined diagnosis is either confirmed or contradicted and the physician's professional opinions on the party's present status and prognosis are developed and presented. No medical treatment of any kind is provided or warranted by the examining physician. The legal requirement of "duty" is not present in this relationship—duty of care or duty of nondisclosure. However, there is a duty of scrupulous objectivity. Under these circumstances any information that the physician derives during the course of the encounter is exempt from the confidentiality doctrine and is, therefore, generally not privileged.

The Promotion and Preservation of the Public Good

A practitioner's legal and ethical duty of nondisclosure is superseded under certain circumstances by the needs and welfare of the public-at-large and/or when statutory provisions require disclosure. The statutes, rules, and regulations regarding disclosure vary widely and extend from the federal level down through the states to county and local municipal governing bodies. These usually involve matters that could have serious implications for public health, safety, and well-being. Epidemics of communicable disease would be an example.

All states require reporting of data entered on birth and death certificates. These documents are in the public domain. In virtually every jurisdiction, reporting of child and elder abuse is required by law. The physician, nurse, and certain other professionals who fail to report instances of such abuse are generally subject to criminal action and possible loss of licensure. Virtually all disclosure statutes provide for immunity from civil lawsuits against those required to report if the disclosure is made in good faith. Likewise, most jurisdictions require the filing of reports with appropriate law enforcement offices regarding the treatment of injuries from gunshot or knife wounds, or other trauma that could be associated with the commission or attempted commission of criminal acts. Statements of intent or threats to commit a criminal act are also reportable.

In certain instances, not directly related to public health and safety yet in the public interest, disclosure may take precedence over an individual's right to privacy. Publication of a significant change in the health status of the president of the United States would fall under this exception as might publication of the names of patients involved in major medical breakthroughs. The courts will not allow any such disclosures to detract from the subjects' dignity.

Disclosure of HIV/AIDS Status

This is arguably related to the exception of qualified privilege. It is a highly controversial issue in medicine, law, and ethics.

Other Disclosure Situations

There are several other situations in which certain patient information might be part of reports or proceedings.

Reports to the Medical Information Bureau

The Medical Information Bureau maintains a database of personal information it receives from over 750 members. These include virtually every major insurance company that issues life, health, and disability insurance in the United States and Canada. Its stated purpose is the prevention of insurance fraud.

If an individual applying for insurance coverage has an existing condition or history of a kind that the insurance business has determined to be "significant to health or longevity," MIB member companies are required to submit a brief, coded report on the applicant to the MIB. At the present time, MIB classifies 210 types of "significant" medical conditions such as hypertension, abnormal EKG readings, and hypercholesterolemia. In addition, they define five nonmedical codes that describe an applicant's personal behavior or lifestyle that relate to possible risk factors.

The individual's medical data, together with certain personal identifiers (name, date and place of birth, occupation, area of current residence) are entered into the MIB database. Presently, it contains over 15 million files. The applicant's Social Security number, home address, and telephone number are not included.

Peer Review and Quality Assurance Activities

Every hospital, nursing home, and other health care provider or institution has a peer review and quality assurance program in place. There are departments and committees in every health care facility. The deliberations and actions of peer review committees are virtually always closed proceedings, and their findings and actions considered privileged and confidential.

State Boards and Professional Organizations

These include both state medical and nursing boards that are charged with licensing various health care providers and professional organizations charged with credentialing members of a profession or a specialty within a profession. State laws vary on requirements of reporting disciplinary actions taken by institutions or peer review bodies. All complaints, reports, and investigatory proceedings of a state board are considered confidential. Full reports of final actions against professional licensure are matters of public record. Virtually all state boards of medicine and nursing maintain records of such licensure actions. Most state medical boards require that malpractice claims, payments, and settlements against physicians be reported. Some state boards require the same for nurses. This information might not be made public.

Reports to the National Practitioner Data Bank

The National Practitioner Data Bank (NPDB) began operations on September 1, 1990, under a federal statute enacted in 1987. At its inception, the concept for the data bank focused primarily on the medical profession, but when eventually implemented, and as amended, the scope of the law included all licensed health care practitioners.

The principal purpose of the NPDB is to compile information and data in an effort to identify and track incompetent and potentially dangerous health care practitioners and to prevent such individuals from easily relocating from state to state and continuing to practice incognito.

The federal statute prescribed mandatory reporting of specified data on selected health care professionals and defines those entities that are required to report. An "entity" is generally defined as any health care organization, professional practice, or professional organization. The law also defines who can access the database, including attorneys. Information on querying, reporting to, and access to the NPDB can be obtained from their web site listed in appendix I.

MENTAL HEALTH AND SUBSTANCE ABUSE RECORDS

Various federal statutes impose strict requirements of confidentiality and rigorous safeguards to protect the records of patients who have been in drug or alcohol treatment or mental health care. Under these statutes, a subpoena may not be sufficient to permit disclosure of such records. The Federal Drug Abuse and Treatment Act of 1972 (21 USC § 1175) requires that any patient records pertaining to treatment for substance abuse are not to be released without a court order. That determination will be made only after the court weighs the risk of harm to the patient against any possible benefit to be derived.

Only a court order will effect release, and then only if the order has been entered in the appropriate manner. Under 42 CFR, Section 2.31, a court order and a subpoena, both of which must specifically refer to and provide for the release of substance abuse records, must be issued in order to authorize disclosure of such records in the absence of patient consent.

In this area of law, as in other areas where there are both federal and state statutes, rules, and regulations that address the same subject matter, federal and state provisions can coexist. Of course, should any conflict arise between these, federal law will prevail.

THE FEDERAL PRIVACY ACT OF 1974

The Federal Privacy Act of 1974 (Public Law 93–579; 5 USC 552a, 88 1896) promotes greater governmental respect for the privacy of citizens. It has been amended eight times since its passage. Section 2, Paragraph 4 of the act states: "The right to privacy is a personal and fundamental right protected by the Constitution of the United States." The phrase "right to privacy" does not appear anywhere in the Constitution. Legal scholars generally agree that the right is implied in that document.

The act requires all *federal* agencies to adopt minimum standards for the collection and processing of personal information and to publish detailed descriptions of these procedures. It also limits the making of such records available to other public and private agencies or parties and requires federal agencies to make the records of a citizen available to them upon his or her request—subject to certain conditions and exclusions. All personal records maintained by any federal agency must be safeguarded in accordance with privacy act procedures.

Objectives of the 1974 Act

The act has four basic policy objectives:

1. To restrict disclosures of personally identifiable records;
2. to grant individuals more rights to access records that agencies maintain on them;

3. to grant individuals the right to seek amendments to agency records maintained on themselves; and
4. to establish a code of "fair information practices" that requires agencies to comply with statutory norms for collection, maintenance, and dissemination of records.

Restrictions

Personal information shall not be collected for inclusion in a record or in a generally available publication unless:

1. The information is collected for a lawful purpose directly related to a function or activity of the collector; and
2. the collection of the information is necessary for, or directly related to, that purpose. Personal information means information or an opinion (including information or an opinion forming part of a database), whether true or not, and whether recorded in a material form or not, about an individual whose identity is apparent, or can reasonably be ascertained, from the information or opinion.

RECENT FEDERAL PROPOSALS REGARDING PRIVACY OF HEALTH CARE RECORDS

At the time this book was being prepared, a comprehensive federal law was being proposed that would protect the privacy of medical records, permit individuals to inspect their own files, and impose sanctions for unauthorized disclosure of such records by hospitals, insurance companies, health maintenance organizations, and pharmaceutical companies. At that time there was no federal law for health records. These have been primarily protected in a somewhat haphazard fashion by state laws. There have been serious deficiencies in enforcement of the laws, rules, and regulations that have been in place.

The proposed federal law would impose greater restrictions on the use of medical records than any state law now in effect. The bill under consideration would establish certain minimum federal standards that would control the flow and use of such information between and among insurance companies and health maintenance organizations in an effort to mitigate the incentives to collect health data on individual citizens and market such information for financial gain. If approved by Congress, the proposals would be the most significant protections for sensitive personal information since the Privacy Act of 1974.

In March 1998, the bill that was being prepared by Senators Robert F.

Bennett (R-Utah) and James M. Jeffords (R-Vermont) would create the first federal protection for health records, imposing criminal penalties for improper disclosure of identifiable records for most nonhealth purposes. Provisions of the bill would include:

- Medical records can be disclosed "for health care, and health care only"—with some exceptions (as will be described).
- Any individual should be permitted to obtain copies of his or her medical record and to correct any information in the record that is inaccurate or incomplete.
- The subject of the medical record will be able to determine who has had prior access to their record and for what reasons.
- Health care institutions will be allowed to use personal health data in the education of physicians and nurses, to carry out research, for utilization and review, and to assess the quality of care provided.
- An employer that might receive such data in the course of approving and/or paying a health insurance or other claim would not be permitted to use such information for any purpose other than that related to the health care of the employee. This would preclude any personnel actions such as transfers, promotions, or terminations based on such information.
- The standards that apply to physicians, hospitals, and other health care providers would apply to insurance companies, pharmaceutical companies, pharmacies, and health care services providers of any kind.
- Criminal penalties will be imposed on any individual who unlawfully discloses confidential medical information and/or attempts to obtain such information by misrepresentation or fraud.

Privacy Issues in Proposed Federal Laws

The Bennet-Jeffords bill would tighten law enforcement access to health records, though not as much as privacy advocates would like. The proposals for such federal regulation are not without their critics. It has been maintained that such uniform standards will facilitate the increasing trend to computerization of personal files and permit the increased, unchecked, and unmonitored flow of such information across state lines—all in the name of "efficient" care. Although the standards being developed may provide for obtaining the consent of the individual before retrieval of his or her record, there is a formidable list of exceptions. These include law enforcement, public health officials, medical researchers, certain health oversight agencies, and health information services to name a few.

Privacy advocates, who, in general, welcome such necessary legislation, were still concerned that it would continue to allow police too much access and prohibit most stronger state laws. Another bill that was being proposed by Senators Patrick J. Leahy (D-Vermont) and Edward M. Kennedy (D-Massachusetts) would require law enforcement officers to obtain a court order before seizing personal records.

There were also concerns about vague language that could allow information to be released to individuals or companies wanting to market products to patients. Coincidentally, the media were reporting at that time that a number of chain supermarket pharmacies and a chain of drugstores were selling prescription information to a marketing company that tracked patients who did not refill their prescriptions at the pharmacies supplying the information.

At that time, the reaction of Congress to such bills was unclear. It remains unclear to this time. Many in Congress favor greater privacy for health care records, but have not addressed the details of the matter. The question will likely be the subject of ongoing intense lobbying by various factions of the health care industry (particularly the AMA and HMOs). Lawmakers are likely to be very wary of antagonizing organizations with substantial financial interests in the access to and use of such information. The AMA has the largest lobbying force in Washington, and spends the largest amount of money in their efforts.

Presently, private health information is being collected, stored, analyzed, and shared with few if any federal safeguards. Protection of the most intimate secrets of millions of patients is erratic at best—dangerous at worst. Donna Shalala, Secretary of Health and Human Services, has affirmed that: "Our private health information is being shared, collected, analyzed and stored with fewer federal safeguards than our video-store records. . . . [A]t present, we rely on a patchwork of state privacy laws, only about a dozen of which are comprehensive. We have no real federal health care privacy standards. We have no national standards" (Pear 1997, A-4). Congress has until mid–1999 to pass legislation; otherwise, the Department of Health and Human Services is free to write its own regulations.

CONFIDENTIALITY ISSUES FOR THE PARALEGAL

At times, in the course of the review and analysis of the record, the paralegal may discover certain facts that are highly personal and sensitive and that may have no relevancy to the issues in the case. These could involve the client's medical or social history, criminal background, or his or her lifestyle or sexual preference. Similar facts may be revealed regarding the client's family members. As a matter of professional ethics, it is imperative that such information be kept confidential and within the confines of the working environment.

The extent to which such information should be included in the final report and summary of the records review will be determined by its relevancy to the issues. If any fact is, or could possibly be, significant, it should be included. If it contributes nothing, it is nothing, and, therefore, should be excluded. If there is any doubt, the reviewer should discuss the matter with the attorney or prepare a separate memo. It must be remembered that the paralegal's summary report could find its way into the hands of individuals who have neither a need to know or right to know such sensitive information.

The paralegal must be constantly aware that the utmost discretion is required in the review and analysis of a client's medical records. As a professional, the paralegal is bound by the guidelines and codes of ethics of the profession—the same ethics that protect the attorney-client privilege. These forbid the unauthorized disclosure of any information about a client that might be derived in the course of investigation and litigation. Among these guidelines and codes are:

- *The Code of Ethics of the National Association of Legal Assistants* (NALA) states in Canon 7: "A legal assistant must protect the confidences of a client, and it shall be unethical for a legal assistant to violate any statute now in effect or hereafter to be enacted controlling privileged communications."
- *The NALA Model Standards and Guidelines for Utilization of Legal Assistants* states in Section V: "Legal assistants should . . . preserve the confidences and secrets of all clients. . . ."
- The National Federation of Paralegal Associations (NPFA) *Model Code of Ethics and Professional Responsibility* states in Canon 5: "A paralegal shall preserve all confidential information provided by the client or acquired from other sources before, during, and after the course of the professional relationship." Subsections EC-5.1 through EC-5.6 of this Canon provide several specific guidelines.
- The American Bar Association's *Model Guidelines for the Utilization of Legal Assistant Services*, Guideline 6: "It is the responsibility of a lawyer to take reasonable measures to ensure that all client confidences are preserved by a legal assistant" (Miller & Urisko 1996, 942–971). [Author's note: This is particularly significant to an attorney who could be liable for a malpractice lawsuit for failure to take such "reasonable measures."]

REFERENCES

American Medical Association, Council on Ethical and Judicial Affairs. 1992. *Principles of Medical Ethics.*

Appleby, Kristyn S., and Joanne Tarver. 1994. *Medical Records Review.* 2d ed. John Wiley & Sons, Inc.

Miller, Roger, and Mary S. Urisko. 1996. *West's Paralegal Today.* West Publishing Co.

Pear, Robert. 1997. Measure would protect medical record privacy. *San Francisco Examiner* (August 10).

7

Contents of the Medical Record

LAWS AND REGULATIONS REGARDING CONTENT

All states require health care institutions to maintain detailed health care provider records in various formats. Federal regulations, such as those dealing with Medicare or Medicaid and those defined by the Department of Health and Human Services, prescribe the form and content of the medical record. As previously noted, JCAHO prescribes specific guidelines in standards and content. Although accreditation by JCAHO is "voluntary," it is necessary to meet the "Conditions of Participation" for Medicare and Medicaid reimbursement. Therefore, although the assortment of documents in medical records varies widely in number and format, they must contain certain information that is common to them all. It must be remembered that more information does not necessarily make a more complete or credible record.

DOCUMENTS IN A TYPICAL MEDICAL RECORD

For any medical record to be complete, it must incorporate sufficient information and other data to identify the subject-patient, confirm and support the medical diagnosis, present the rationale for the treatment regimen prescribed, and completely document the care given and identify those health care providers involved.

The number and type of documents will be determined by the circumstances that gave rise to the compilation of the record. A patient's record derived over a long period of hospitalization for a complex illness and treatment regimen will be much larger and varied than that of someone treated over a short course of time for a relatively minor injury, illness, or surgical procedure. The patient's response to treatment and the prognosis will also be factors.

The source of the medical record—hospital or physician—will be a determining factor as will any prior history of hospitalization or physician care. "Hospital records differ from records from a doctor's office in a number of ways. They are frequently more complete, because a hospital may require each physician to complete a variety of forms and papers in order to use the hospital for patients. In addition, there are records of physicians' orders to the pharmacy and nursing staff, separate records by the nursing staff, and records from the operating room if surgery is performed" (Johnson and Wolfe 1995, 5).

An extensive list of those documents that might be found in any record is included in appendix III. The particular documents that might be included will, of course, vary considerably according to the nature and severity of the patient's illness, the complexity of the medical regimen involved, the prognosis, and the individual's and family's response to the health care provided.

Certain documents will be common to virtually all records. Additional documents would be included where the patient is admitted for trauma or other emergency treatment or surgery. These standard records would usually include:

- A face sheet: This admission form contains basic patient information, including his or her name, address, telephone number, names of next-of-kin, religion, insurance coverage, and other data.
- Preadmission records, if any: These would include all records of prehospitalization care, preadmission test reports, and approvals.
- An advance directive—a "living will." Inclusion is not required, but if one has been executed, the patient should provide it for inclusion.
- Conditions of admission: An admission form that the patient signs to confirm his or her expressed consent to "routine" care. (It usually affirms that the institution does not guarantee the outcome.)
- Special consents: These would include any informed consents, that is, those required for any nonroutine diagnostic or therapeutic procedure.
- Authorization for release of information: This authorizes the release of the patient's record to certain entities. These might include Blue Cross/Blue Shield, Medicare/Medicaid, HMOs, and insurance companies.

- A history and physical (H&P): This will incorporate a physical examination (PE). This provides baseline data to assist in a diagnosis, and includes a review of systems (ROS) and signs observed. The patient's past medical history (PMH), which may be useful in establishing a tentative or provisional diagnosis.
- A family history including relatives with similar medical problems, causes of death, and any other relevant data. Social history—including such information as personal lifestyle and habits.
- Statement of the patient's current chief complaint (symptoms) and a statement of the physician's findings (diagnosis, or "impression").
- Proposed plan of treatment—general or specific.
- Physicians' orders: These are written instructions to nursing and ancillary services and other physicians regarding all medications and treatments. Their purpose is to communicate the plan of care to all other members of health care team. These orders include:
  1. admission,
  2. ongoing,
  3. pre- and postoperative—where surgery is indicated, and
  4. discharge.
- Physicians' progress notes:

  A daily chronological narrative relating to the patient's diagnosis, course of treatment, response to the medical regimen, and the patient's ongoing status up to and including the time of discharge.
- Nurses notes: These will include:
  1. An admission history and physical assessment by a nurse,
  2. nursing care plans (these may or may not be in record), including *nursing* orders based on *nursing* diagnoses,
  3. flow sheets, various check lists, graphic sheets,
  4. medication administration records (MAR),
  5. miscellaneous nursing reports—for example, flow sheets in specialty units such as ICU, CCU—and
  6. nurses' progress notes: These will be the most detailed progress notes in the chart. They describe all care given by the nursing staff. They should confirm the implementation of the physicians' orders. They will detail nursing assessments including the patient's physical and emotional status.

- Laboratory reports
- Reports of other diagnostic tests and procedures
- Discharge summary and discharge planning and teaching including:
  1. A discharge summary of all treatment during hospital stay,
  2. an evaluation of the patient's response to treatment,
  3. confirmation of physicians' final diagnosis,
  4. an outline of the discharge plan including a follow-up care regimen, and
  5. a statement of the patient's condition at time of discharge

BASIC PATIENT INFORMATION

Of all the documents, obviously the most important are those that provide basic data about the patient. Every chart must contain enough information for any health care provider unfamiliar with the patient to provide appropriate care. This should include physiological information, therapeutic information, and any special patient characteristics such as allergies or handicaps. This information is usually summarized on a cover sheet. There are various formats for this summarization, but they should provide a means to immediately identify abnormal findings and all significant medical problems that require attention.

In clinics or in the offices of medical practices with a number of physicians, the variety of documents in a medical record begin to resemble those of a hospital medical record. All of the physicians in the health care setting must record data in the same format and record sufficient data to assure that any other physician on the health care team will be able to provide effective, consistent, and therapeutic care and be able to identify ongoing or new problems. The objective is to ensure the maximum degree of efficiency and continuity of therapeutic care.

The hospital setting, or multiphysician clinics or practices can create a risk that significant data could be overlooked in a sharing of responsibility for a patient's care. There usually is one physician in charge of the patient's overall care, and the chart should identify this physician. The chart would routinely be referred to this physician for review whenever the patient is treated by another practitioner. This review allows the primary physician to assess the care of other providers and confirm that it is in accordance with the medical regimen prescribed. The reviewing physician can then add his or her comments or other notes as necessary to ensure that the next provider who encounters that particular patient has complete, accurate, and current information to assure continuity of care. This should be confirmed as having been done in the course of review and analysis of the medical record.

REFERENCE

Johnson, Diann, and Sidney M. Wolfe. 1995. *Medical Records: Getting Yours*. Public Citizen's Health Research Group.

8

Altered or Tampered Records

LEGAL IMPLICATIONS OF AN ALTERED MEDICAL RECORD

Tampering is illicit altering. It is wrongfully adding to, deleting, or otherwise changing information or data that is already contained in a medical record. Additions might be made to complete or clarify. But no matter the intent, any such alterations could be interpreted as tampering unless fully documented reasons and explanations accompany the changes.

Any note or other document in a medical record that has been amended and/or corrected in some way is one that has been altered. The converse may not be the case if the intent is not to amend and clarify but to deceive and conceal. Any attempt to deliberately falsify a record can be evidence in law of the concept of "consciousness of negligence." The inference could be that the person who altered the record was well aware of his or her own negligence, and that this act of alteration was an attempt to conceal it. In such a situation, a judge may instruct a jury that negligence on the part of the defendant can be presumed from the defendant's obvious attempt to hide it—even though no other evidence of their negligence is present.

If the entire medical record has gone missing, this could be extremely damaging to the plaintiff's case. It would call into question both the quality of care that he or she had received and the integrity of both the providers of that care and the institution itself.

If the defendant had destroyed records under a consciousness of negligence and guilt, such consciousness would be relevant to causation.

"[W]hen a defendant's negligence makes it impossible for the plaintiff to prove proximate cause, it is more appropriate to hold the defendant liable than to deny an innocent plaintiff recovery" (Appleby and Tarver 1997, 68).

The deliberate *omission* of significant information or data is also tampering. The unauthorized removal and/or destruction of any document in the record could make the entire record suspect. If any document must be revised or rewritten, the original must remain intact as part of the record. A jury might conclude that the document that was destroyed could have been incriminating, and might consider such an action to have been an attempt to conceal evidence. If this was in fact the intent, the individual responsible has committed fraud.

Tampering as Fraud

If the attorney for the plaintiff can prove that there had been any attempt to alter, tamper with, or falsify any document in the client's record in an attempt to conceal the facts, the attorney will claim fraud and conspiracy to commit fraud on the part of the defendant(s). If this can be proven, it is the *kiss of death* for the defendant's case.

Any attempt to conceal or manipulate facts with a deliberate, willful intent to interfere with a legal inquiry, mislead, misinform, or otherwise deceive in any way to avoid blame constitutes fraud. In a case of malpractice it could be considered a *criminal* offense—a *felony*. A defendant in a civil malpractice action found to have perpetrated a fraud could become a defendant in a criminal action. Otherwise, in a number of states, based on the intent, degree, and circumstances, certain acts of inappropriate alteration of a medical record may be treated as a misdemeanor crime of one degree or another. As noted in a previous chapter, *fraud can extend the statute of limitations indefinitely*!

Attorneys' Concerns with a Medical Record

"Another source of altered records might be the opposing party's attorney. . . . [W]hen copies of records are provided by a plaintiff's attorney, documents that are considered 'unrelated' to the subject accident might have been removed. This is done with the honest intention of protecting the client's privacy, but can be circumvented by obtaining, through subpoena or authorization, for a complete set of records" (Appleby and Tarver 1994, 187).

Both the plaintiff's and defendant's attorneys will be concerned with integrity of the medical record—albeit for different reasons.

> Medical records are the cornerstone of a medical malpractice case, relied on by the parties and their expert witnesses to prove or disprove the existence of negligence. When key records are altered or destroyed, the plaintiff's ability to make a *prima facie* case for negligence is greatly hampered or disappears altogether. Alteration or destruction of records can have disastrous results for the defendant too. An individual who alters records in an attempt to control the outcome of a proceeding will often find those actions ultimately determined in the plaintiff's favor, despite other evidence that might have supported the defendant's legal defense absent the altered records.
>
> The spoliation of or attempt to suppress material evidence by a party provides sufficient reason for an inference of guilt or negligence by that misconduct. Courts will not allow parties to benefit from their own misconduct. . . . The evidentiary presumption against a party acting in a deceitful matter is called the *spoliation doctrine*. The destruction must be shown to be the result of negative intent or bad faith; negligence alone will not justify the inference that the defendant knew his or her case was weak and could not be won otherwise. (Appleby and Tarver 1997, 66–67)

Spoliation: Legal Theories and Consequences

The tort of spoliation requires that several elements be present:

1. Pending or probable litigation involving the plaintiff;
2. knowledge by the defendant of the pending litigation;
3. intentional acts of spoliation by the defendant designed to disrupt the plaintiff's case;
4. actual disruption of the plaintiff's case; and
5. damages to the plaintiff proximately caused by the defendant's acts or actions.

SIGNS OF ALTERATION OR TAMPERING

In reviewing and analyzing each of the documents in a record, the examiner will look for any signs of tampering. These include:

- Significant changes in content of any information or data;
- expansion of an original entry, particularly if this contains an "ex-

planation," "clarification," self-serving rationale, or any other "sanitization" of the original entry;

- the alteration or obliteration of any entries in any way so as to make the original entry unreadable;
- corrections made at different times than the original entry perhaps with different pens or ink color or different handwriting;
- overwritten entries or additions written on the margins;
- changes in the timing of entries—especially when they are coincident with and crucial to the events alleged in the malpractice claim;
- inconsistencies in dates and times of entries;
- an excess number of late entries and/or addenda involving the events, individuals, or circumstances surrounding the alleged incident of malpractice and the resulting claim;
- the addition of, or removal of, entire pages.

If records are usually handwritten, insertion of a dictated note should be questioned. Conversely, a handwritten note in a series of dictated notes could be suspect. As previously discussed, the medical record is a business record and evidence of its credibility will derive from the appearance that it has been maintained in the regular course of business. Anything that may indicate special treatment or handling of a record could make it suspect. Even an alteration that appears to be of no significance might bring the entire record into question.

The most inconsequential action, such as the inadvertent loss of only a single document in a voluminous record, could be interpreted as an attempt to hide something and cause a jury to speculate on what else might be missing—accidentally or otherwise.

Possible Motives for Tampering

There are a number of "untoward" events that might occur and that might provoke an individual (culpable or not) to attempt to "edit" his or her notes. These usually occur during the patient's hospitalization, but the attempt might also be made at any time after the patient has been discharged.

1. There might have been a medical or surgical "misadventure" or "maloccurance" (the common euphemisms). These can occur during routine surgery or obstetrical procedures, or can be the result of any procedure with an actual or potentially adverse outcome.

2. It may be done in anticipation of another practitioner assuming the medical management of a patient where criticism of the previous regimen of care could be warranted.
3. The sudden and unanticipated demise of a patient, particularly if it could be deemed a "wrongful" death that could prompt a suit.
4. It may occur during preparation of the discharge summary when unfavorable or compromising details might be omitted for the sake of "brevity."
5. When a practitioner is made aware of the plaintiff's attorney's request for a copy of the medical record, he or she may panic at the thought of a possible threat of a lawsuit and attempt to retrieve the patient's file from the medical records department without realizing that it is too late for damage control, or the legal implications of such a futile attempt.

Institutional Methods of Preventing Tampering

Hospitals generally have written policies and procedures in place to shield medical records from alterations. These are developed and implemented according to regulations prescribed by JCAHO. There is no such watchdog in a physician's office. The physician is bound by personal and professional ethics and standards.

Most hospitals have a risk management department that investigates and manages malpractice claims and lawsuits. At the first indication of a potential suit, the risk manager will generally obtain and secure the entire medical record and any other documents or items associated with it. By doing so, the facility will be better able to protect itself from any eventual accusations that the records or other evidence were inappropriately accessed and possibly altered.

Once a discharged patient's file is consigned to the medical records department, it should not be allowed to leave the department. The exception would be if that particular patient is readmitted to the hospital. Routinely, all relevant original records of prior hospitalization are sent to the unit to which the individual has now been readmitted. This effectively makes old files available for, and susceptible to, alteration—a highly unlikely event. Ideally, copies of all relevant documents should be supplied rather than the originals. However, this procedure is not feasible, expedient, or economical and is simply not done. Urgency of a clinical situation may demand that an entire original record be brought to the floor immediately.

To prevent loss or compromise of any part of a record, or one as a whole, medical records departments are encouraged to enforce policies that forbid a file to be "checked out" by anyone. Rather, areas should be set aside for the convenience of an authorized reviewer. Even if effective mechanisms are in place, there is likely to be no feasible way to determine if a record that has been accessed inside or outside of the department remains intact. Someone would have to sit at the elbow of the reviewer at all times and never let the documents out of his or her sight.

Under no circumstances should a practitioner be permitted to retrieve a record from the medical record department files and attempt to make any alterations by him-or herself. It must be remembered that long before a lawsuit is actually filed the plaintiff's attorney may have already obtained a copy of the complete record, and this has been reviewed in detail by an attorney, a paralegal, or a litigation consultant. Any discrepancies that are later identified (especially before a skeptical jury) may impeach the entire record and certainly the credibility of the defendant.

A physician or a nurse can never arbitrarily add to, change, or rewrite another's notes. If a practitioner determines that this has occurred, he or she should have referred the matter to the facility's administration. Inevitably alterations to a medical record must be made. These can be as routine as correcting spelling, grammar, or mistranscribed data; or they can involve substantive errors such as missing orders, omitted assessments, or absent progress notes.

If any *significant* alteration must be made in a patient's record beyond a reasonable time period, the practitioner is usually required to advise the institution's administration in writing of their need and intent. When and if approved, the physician or nurse must proceed with the addendum according to the policies and procedures established by the institution's risk management department. Any other person who might have relied on the original record must be advised of the revision in a timely manner.

What to Do If Tampering Is Suspected

If the paralegal identifies any possible sign of alteration during the review and analysis, he or she should advise the attorney immediately. The paralegal, or the layperson, should make arrangements with the custodian to review the original documents. It is advised that he or she take the "as produced" copy of the record along. The paralegal should also take the list of the records that the attorney had originally requested from the custodian. The original chart may not be arranged in the same order as the copy received. This is particularly true if the copy was received from a document retrieval service that may have rearranged it to its needs or procedures in preparation and reproduction.

The signs of tampering outlined previously are usually evident from a careful reading of the documents. A reviewer will examine the records for these signs as best as he or she can. Suggestions and guidelines for the detailed review and analysis of specific documents that may facilitate the detection of tampering, and the preparation a chronological summary of the events, will be presented in chapter 10.

If there is any suspicion of a document having been altered using an undetectable method that could conceal the original entry from the lay examiner, the expert opinion—derived from sophisticated examination techniques—of a forensic document examiner may be required.

FORENSIC DOCUMENT EXAMINATION

If there is any suggestion or question of tampering, a forensic document examiner may have to be brought in to examine the *original* records. It is his or her function to review all questionable documents and provide independent, scientific evidence of their integrity, reliability, and validity. Copies can be utilized for an initial evaluation, that is, writing style, grammar, syntax, consistencies in corrections, a writer's handwriting itself, and a comparison of handwriting. However, copies are limited in the subtle details they can capture from the original.

The original document will be the subject of highly sophisticated scientific scrutiny and testing. The forensic expert will be able to detect any effort to subvert a record. The expert will note any and all of the signs of tampering outlined previously, but will also employ a variety of scientific instruments and procedures in a laboratory examination and analysis to detect covert attempts to change any part of the record—from a single word to entire pages.

Forensic Document Examination Techniques

The forensic document examiner can employ several scientific techniques in evaluating medical records. These include: (1) infrared reflectance photography, (2) infrared luminescence photography, (3) X-rays, (4) electrostatic detection, (5) stereomicroscopy, (6) laser technology, and (7) chromatography.

Both infrared photography tests can graphically demonstrate differences in writing instruments that may appear to be the same to a casual examination. These tests are nondestructive. They produce a photograph that a jury can easily interpret. Some inks will seem to disappear on infrared reflectance. In infrared luminescence photographs, certain inks are recorded as white images on a black background. An X-ray of a document will disclose an original entry on a substrate that has been obliterated by any type of correction fluid.

The most significant piece of scientific equipment used is electrostatic detection apparatus (ESDA). This is a method of detecting any indented writing on the surface of an underlying document resulting from writing on a page overlaying it. The "latent impressions" are revealed on the underlying page. This technique is particularly valuable in determining if any pages have been removed and rewritten. It can also can establish when a particular note or portion of a note was originally written. It is useful only if the overlaying page had not been removed from the record and written on separately, in which case there could, of course, be no impressions transferred to a substratal page.

Paper can be identified by manufacturer and date of manufacture. Ink "tagging" can establish the earliest date of availability of inks used in a record. Most ink manufactures in the United States are involved in a federal government program that prescribes an annual "forced formula change" of ink on January 1. One use is to allow the Internal Revenue Service to identify backdated documents (Hart 1994, 19–20).

Original documents produced by typewriters or computer printers of any kind will be examined to determine specific elements such as the manufacturer of the machine, fonts, sizes of type face, pitch, impression, and other details specific to any given type of typewriter or printer. This will determine if all pages of a document were reproduced by the same machine—at the same time.

The analytic and testing procedures used by the forensic examiner can be either nondestructive or destructive of the material being tested. In the event of a destructive test, a court order may be required, even though only a minute sample of the suspect document (possible evidence) might be required.

REFERENCES

Appleby, Kristyn S., and Joanne Tarver. 1997. *Medical Records Review*. 2d ed. *Cumulative Supplement*. John Wiley & Sons.

Appleby, Kristyn S., and Joanne Tarver. 1994. *Medical Records Review*. 2d ed. John Wiley & Sons, Inc.

Hart, Linda J. 1994. Alterations to medical records can be detected. *Professional Medical Assistant* (November/December): 19–20.

9

Preparing for the Review

APPROACHES TO A REVIEW OF MEDICAL RECORDS

The two most common situations that will require the review of a medical record are cases of: (1) personal injury and (2) medical or nursing malpractice. Each situation requires a somewhat different approach to the process of review and analysis.

Personal Injury

In a personal injury case, the claimant was injured in some way before being admitted to a hospital—before becoming a patient. The patient and his or her attorney already know when, where, how, and possibly why the injury occurred and who, they assert, is to blame. In these instances, the reviewer will examine the record to determine:

- What was the nature and of extent of the injury sustained;
- what treatments were given or procedures carried out;
- who provided treatment, who performed the procedures;
- how did the victim tolerate the treatment (pain and suffering?);
- what is the prognosis—to what degree will the person recover;
- will there be any disability—temporary or permanent—or any disfigurement?

In personal injury cases, the review may involve only a relatively small number of specific records, and it may be possible to obtain and utilize only these rather than a complete, voluminous file. The reviewer's primary task here is to prepare a description of the injuries and course of medical treatment, including rehabilitation, rather than an evaluation of the quality of care per se. This does not preclude the need for scrutiny of the record for any evidence of possible malpractice during the course of care.

Malpractice

In a malpractice suit, the plaintiff claims that his or her injury occurred during a course of treatment by a physician or nurse, before or after admission to the hospital, and that the alleged injury was the result of professional negligence. Or the claim may be that he or she was harmed after being released from the hospital as a result of a premature discharge and/or inadequate preparation for proper and therapeutic care at home—by the patient him-or herself or by caregivers.

The reviewer's task here is to determine and prepare a description of:

- What happened—what are the details of the alleged incident;
- how did it happen—the plaintiff's version versus the account documented in the record (if any);
- what could have been the cause;
- could there be any other causes;
- when did it happen;
- where did it happen;
- who was involved;
- who could have been the cause;
- who was present—who could be possible witnesses;
- what was the nature and degree of the injury claimed;
- what was the patient's reaction;
- what is the prognosis—to what degree will the patient recover;
- will there be any disability—temporary or permanent—or any disfigurement?

In a personal injury case, many of these facts are already on record. The causes of the injury per se are not the focus of the review, but rather the injury itself and its implications for the patient. In malpractice, ascertaining such facts and the exact cause of the injury, as far as is possible, will be the objective. The reviewer assumes the role of detective or investigator and conducts the analysis with a suspicious, skeptical, questioning methodology. He or she will compare the plaintiff's assertions against the documentation in the record—all this while maintaining as objective an approach as possible.

THE REVIEWER'S TASKS

The paralegal's or layperson's review and analysis will entail a detailed examination of all relevant documents that may be included in the file, as well as those that are not included and must be obtained. Appendix III lists those documents that might be contained in any given medical record. In chapter 10 a checklist format will be outlined that can be used to define various points and/or questions during the course of the review of individual documents or groups of documents. This will expedite the process by helping to organize the documents according to content. From that point, the analysis of the content can begin.

Determine the Facts and Issues of the Case

Before beginning the formal review and analysis, it is essential that the reviewer *educate himself or herself about the case*! He or she must define, as precisely as possible, *what* he or she is looking for. Both the paralegal and the layperson should also review: (1) the required elements of malpractice, (2) the statue of limitations in medical malpractice in their state of jurisdiction, and (3) the relevant rules of evidence.

One can not expect to conduct a thorough review and analysis and prepare a meaningful summary without adequate knowledge of the basic legal principles, the allegations, and the issues involved in the case—*all* of the issues—the obvious as well as the potential. There is no better preparation for reviewing medical records than to become very familiar with the case, the parties, the issues, the witnesses—all of the facts available. Unless all of these are known, significant, relevant information might be discounted or could be overlooked entirely. Understanding all of the medical-legal issues specific to the allegations will allow the reviewer to assign priorities to the materials in planning, organizing, and carrying out the process of review and preparing a summary report.

A paralegal should *never* let the attorney be surprised by any potentially harmful information that he or she may have overlooked. Before beginning, the paralegal should ask:

1. Why do we have this case?
2. What type of case is it?
3. What are the issues and allegations?
4. What should I be looking for?

5. Where should I look?
6. How far, how long, should I look?

If the reviewer is not familiar with the complaint, the pleadings, and the factual allegations, he or she should begin by reviewing any that may be available. This should include an examination of all correspondence and pleadings. This is most important. Failure to do so will compromise an understanding of the issues and questions that must be addressed. (Ideally, the paralegal should be a participant in the initial interview of the client.) If interrogatories are available, both the questions and any available responses should be studied.

The reviewer should have a general understanding of the type of medical problem or injury the plaintiff is alleging. The specifics will come from the detailed review and analysis of their record. For the moment, the highly technical details and medical language can be deferred for further explanation and interpretation, possibly by a testifying or a consulting expert.

It should be determined who referred the plaintiff to the treating physician or other health care provider. Was he or she sent to this practitioner by an attorney? Is there any evidence that the plaintiff was "shopping" for a physician or medical opinion that was most favorable to his or her case? Insurance companies, particularly workers' compensation carriers, maintain files on attorneys and physicians who "collaborate" or "specialize" in such cases.

If any of the issues are not clear, they should be discussed with the attorney before beginning the review and analysis process. The paralegal should determine if there are any particular areas that the attorney suggests they focus on. Does the attorney have any questions or suspicions? What are they? Does the paralegal have any questions or suspicions? Have these been discussed with the attorney?

Confirm That the Medical Record Is Complete

How will a reviewer know if any records are missing? The review itself might involve close scrutiny of only certain records. An attorney may initially request only these to save time and money. The layperson could be at a disadvantage here in not being able to identify those particular documents that might be most relevant and thus incurring a needless expense in having the entire record copied.

Before beginning, there are several points that must be considered. These questions may not be answerable until the review is well under way or possibly only after it has been completed. At the outset, however, the reviewer should ask:

- Do I have everything I need to start?
- Does the medical record, "as-produced" and in hand, appear complete?
- Could there be any additional records?
- Have all the documents requested in the attorney's letter of request been received?
- Do any essential documents or records appear to be absent? From the list of records in appendix III the reviewer should be able to identify certain documents that *must* be included. Are any of these missing? What are they? Where are they? How can they be obtained?
- Are there any other known records of a past medical history, previous hospitalizations, treatments? Could these be relevant? Where are they?
- Have there been any follow-up treatments? All postdischarge records, if any, must be obtained to determine the patient's current status, diagnosis, the degree and extent of residual injuries and impairment, and prognosis.

As the in-depth review and analysis proceeds, the analyst should note any cross-references to other documents. These should be checked to confirm that each of the documents cited is in the file. Frequently, certain ancillary records may not need to be obtained initially. These might include fetal monitor strips, X-rays, EKG and EEG strips, pathology slides, and a variety of others that may or may not be relevant. For the moment, the focus should be on the essential records. The review and analysis may identify other key records to be obtained.

If it is cost effective and the record is not too voluminous, the paralegal should prepare a working copy for him-or herself and the attorney. The as-produced set can be maintained exactly as received from the custodian. The lay reviewer is not likely to need an extra copy, but it may be advisable to make one in the event that he or she would find it necessary to include selected, unannotated documents in any correspondence.

Paginate the Record

It is strongly advised that the entire record be paginated. This is a must. To carry out an effective and thorough review, every page should be numbered before the start. For attorneys and paralegals, this will ensure uniformity and consistency in citations and references to specific documents in a record comprised of groups of documents with the same title or description, for example progress notes that could consist of hundreds of pages. Ideally, all parties will have the same numbers on the same pages.

In the process of copying and handling, pages can become mixed up and out of order. As soon as the records have been received, it should be confirmed that they are paginated. Many document retrieval and copying companies that provide services to the legal community will paginate documents during the copying process. They will usually number stamp the bottom of the page.

For the lay person, penciled-in page numbers will be invaluable in reading through the pile of documents and keeping track of where relevant information is found. This can be a beginning frame of reference. It will confirm that the reviewer has a certain number of pages but *not necessarily all of the record*. Pagination can be done before or after the record is organized and categorized by type of document.

Organize and Categorize the Documents

Organizing the documents is an essential step before beginning any review. There may be no need to organize, or even obtain, the entire record for an initial screening. This may not be cost effective. This decision may be made following the preliminary screening, which is discussed in chapter 10. At this time, the number of available records may be limited. As the review and the pretrial preparation of the case proceed, the volume of documents could increase markedly.

The reviewer's task will be to assemble the documents in such a way as to facilitate and expedite the review process. The challenge will be to take all the relevant information contained in the stack of documents and turn it into a concise, informative, functional summary for use either as an attorney work product or as a personal reference.

The reviewer may elect to categorize the documents for easier management of the file. This would involve sorting and grouping all records into folders by subject or by type of information or data. This should be basically the same arrangement as the patient's chart as it was originally compiled and utilized by a health care facility's staff in the clinical setting where a consistent order of documents is essential for immediate reference. Charts are usually maintained in this same order by the medical records department of the facility. However, in the process of copying and preparation for delivery, the documents can become a jumble. The challenge may be to sort the whole mess out and put it back into some semblance of order. The list of documents in appendix III may assist in this.

As the organization and categorization proceeds, the reviewer should attempt to concentrate on, identify, and segregate those documents that appear relevant to the claims and issues of the case. Documents with possible significant content can be tabbed with stick-on notes or a list of their page numbers can be compiled. This will facilitate a personal review and, later, that of an attorney, expert consultant, and expert witness.

When the documents are identified, grouped, and subgrouped in *chronological* order, one can then begin to review, analyze, and summarize them according to their relevance, significance, and priority. At any stage of the organization or review, a continuing effort should made to determine if there are any significant and pertinent records missing. What are they? Where are they? Must they be obtained?

There is no one right way to organize and review a medical record—there are different techniques for different types of records and types of cases. Over time, the paralegal will develop a facility for expeditious and effective review and the preparation of concise, meaningful summaries. The lay reviewer might be confused and confounded in the initial encounter with documents written in a "foreign" language. Organization, patience, and the availability of useful references will get them through. A logical, systematic methodology applied to the process will make the task easier and produce the best results. No matter what the means, meaningful results are the end.

10

The Review and Analysis of the Documents in a Medical Record

THE REVIEW

When a medical record is obtained through a signed authorization, request for production of documents, subpoena, or some other means, the reviewer's task is to organize the documents, carry out an analysis of them, and prepare a summary report of the findings.

In a personal injury or malpractice case, time and budgetary constraints may dictate how a paralegal or attorney undertakes the review. The lay reviewer may not have such limitations. In either instance, the individual may wish to begin with a quick preliminary examination prior to undertaking a detailed, in-depth analysis, or he or she may elect to forego the preliminary survey and plunge in.

Preliminary Screening

The medical record may be relatively small or quite voluminous. Regardless, there are certain documents that usually provide the answers to critical questions. If the record is not too voluminous, the reviewer may wish to read it through beginning to end, not taking extensive notes or inserting a large number of tabs.

At this stage, the reviewer need *not* read *every* page and *every* detail. Do not try to pick up every point or every fact at this time. That will be done in the course of the detailed analysis of the documents that is discussed later in this chapter. Quickly survey all of the materials at hand and attempt to identify any that could be relevant to the incident. Focus on the most significant, the most pertinent. This initial, cursory screening will provide quick overview—an idea of how the content of the record is organized, how it flows, what documents are in it, and where specific information might be found.

Brief annotations can be made and those documents that could be of significance can be tabbed for later scrutiny. Stick-on notes are ideal for this—but put the *page number* on each one! Always include a page number in each annotation or reference; this will aid in cross-referencing, indexing, searching, and retrieval. Whenever possible, a computer word-processing program should be used in annotating the medical record. Group all notes and any questions by source documents and page number.

This initial, cursory review may not provide all—or any—of the answers. The most important thing is to know what answers are *not* known at the time and *where* they might eventually be found. The payoff is finding that one pertinent note or document that can make or break the case. This can occur at any point in any level of review no matter how brief or prolonged the process. The reviewer may find it immediately, it may take hours or days, or it may not be there at all.

Having read the record through, the reviewer should now be better able to organize and categorize the documents in anticipation of a detailed examination. A brief summary report prepared at this time can be in narrative form without all of the details surrounding the events, but specific to the event or alleged incident of injury.

At any point in the review process, continue to be alert to the possibility of any missing records. Note any records that are referred to in the medical record and that would be relevant to the issues but are not in hand. Obtain these.

Assessing Documents for Legibility

Simply reading many of the documents can be confounding. In both the initial screening and the formal review and analysis, one of the greatest challenges will be the quality of the copy and the legibility of the documents in it. Poor copies may be the best available. The paralegal may photocopy any illegible portions and attach them to their summary, leaving the attorney to decipher them.

If illegible records and indecipherable handwriting present a problem, if the copies are of such poor overall quality as to be useless, or if any erasures or other tampering is suspected, the original should be examined. If a particular record seems critical to the issues of the case, the reviewer will have to locate, examine, and copy the original document. It will be necessary to contact the custodian to determine if a better copy can be obtained or if the original could be made available for comparison and clarification and to confirm the custodian's procedures and requirements for access.

The reviewer is advised to first read what he or she can. This tactic may eventually help in deciphering other entries. Often the notes of one provider will mimic those of another who's handwriting is difficult to interpret. This may provide the reviewer with clues. The content should never be guessed at or a meaning assumed. If the reviewer can not read everything, he or she should not let themselves get bogged down.

If he or she believes the document to be significant, a handwriting expert may eventually have to be consulted. At some point in discovery or at a trial, the person who wrote the illegible note may be asked to decipher it. In the event of a trial, illegible handwriting can work to a plaintiff's advantage when sloppy penmanship will be equated with sloppy patient care. Of course, a physician or nurse named as a defendant can always be queried by his or her own counsel to clarify an entry.

THE IN-DEPTH REVIEW

The purpose of this review is to gain a *comprehensive* idea of all of the events, issues and claims in the case and prepare a comprehensive summary report of these in a logical, chronological order. It will involve a detailed comparison of the record's content to the allegations and claims and the correlation of that content with all discovery materials. The final report should confirm the presence or absence of at least three of the elements of malpractice—duty, injury, and causation. A most important purpose is to determine the need for, and qualifications of, any expert witnesses required to attest to the standards of care and the fourth element—breach of duty.

The paralegal's report will also contribute to drafting and responding to interrogatories, responding to or preparing requests for document production, and identifying all possible witnesses and other defendants.

The review will involve an analysis of all relevant documents to answer all relevant questions. However, the focus will be on any of those documents that may provide the information that is critical to the allegations and issues, those that will provide the answers to:

- When did each significant event occur? Note specifically when the incident of injury or alleged malpractice took place—exact dates, times.
- Where did it happen—the patient's room, the operating room?
- Who was involved? Who was present? Who were the witnesses? Who else could have been involved? Who else could be a possible defendant?
- What treatments or procedures were involved?
- Who ordered them?

- Why were they ordered?
- Who performed them?
- What happened? What transpired according to the written record as compared to the statements of the patient/plaintiff or others?
- What was the outcome? Was there, in fact, an injury?
- Why and how did it happen? What were the *apparent* causes?
- Could there have been negligence or was it simply an accident?
- If there appears to be negligence, who may have been negligent?

CHECKLISTS FOR THE REVIEW AND ANALYSIS OF INDIVIDUAL DOCUMENTS IN A MEDICAL RECORD

As previously noted, the review will involve a detailed analysis of all relevant documents to answer all relevant questions or clarify all possibly significant points as outlined. It will include an interpretation of the scientific or technical language and a description of treatments, procedures, and medications.

To conduct the review effectively and efficiently, the documents are grouped by major category and a suggested check list and/or discussion is presented for each. These checklists will be applicable primarily to malpractice cases. It is a reasonably inclusive list; however, each and every question or point will not be relevant in each and every review. The individual analyst will determine the relevant guidelines to apply, questions to ask, and points to raise. Certainly, not all questions will be answerable from this or any other checklist. The review process can sometimes raise more questions than it can answer. Pursuing these answers can be an ongoing challenge.

THE DOCUMENTS

The documents in the following checklist format are listed in the order in which they might be arranged in a typical medical record in use in a clinical setting and maintained by a medical records department.

It may seem so elementary as to not need mentioning, but the reviewer must confirm that a *patient's name* appears on *each and every document* in the medical record, and that name should be recorded by an embossing plate or other marking equipment. Any document with a written patient identification could be suspect.

The Policy and Procedure Manual

There are frequent references in this chapter to the "policies and procedure" (P&P) and the P&P manual. The reviewer may have to obtain the relevant references from the institution's manual to answer a number of questions of conformity to P&P that may arise from the notes. *Note*: The reference must be to those policies or procedures that were in effect *at the time of the incident.*

Intake and Admission Documents, Including the History and Physical

- Check the "Face Sheet" for all essential information, including the patient's name, address, telephone number, next-of-kin, religion, insurance coverage, and other essential data. Is all of the information correct? Is the patient's name spelled correctly—consistently?
- Review any preadmission/prehospitalization care records, reports, and approvals—including any treating physician's office records and any clinic records.
- Examine the "Conditions of Admission" statement. This should indicate that the patient had consented to receive basic, routine care and that the institution did not guarantee the outcome. This is usually shown on the reverse side of the admission/discharge form.
- Was the admission assessment completed within a reasonable time or the within the prescribed time if that is indicated?
- Was a history and physical (H&P) done by a physician? The physical examination (PE) provides baseline data to assist in a preliminary diagnosis. It includes a review of systems (ROS) and signs observed and symptoms stated by the patient. (If not already required, the reviewer may now find a need to start referring to appendix IV to assist in interpreting abbreviations.)
- What are the details of the patient's current chief complaint as he or she stated it in his or her own words?
- Review the statement of "findings." What was the admitting diagnosis? What was ruled out? What was the rationale? Is the admitting diagnosis relevant to the alleged injury in any way?
- Review the past medical history (PMH). Are there any references to any preexisting conditions relevant to the injuries now claimed in the suit?
- Could the present claim be an exacerbation of a preexisting problem?
- Review the patient's family history including close relatives with similar medical histories. Review the patient's social history, their

personal lifestyle, habits, and other factors. Note any particularly high-risk behaviors, or occupations—past or present.

- Who carried out the assessment? The history and physical should have been done by a physician. A registered nurse (RN) usually does a basic assessment after admission to a unit. Compare these two documents.
- Was an RN required to complete an assessment at the time of admission to a nursing unit? Did an LPN or nursing assistant do any part of it?
- Did the intake assessment or H&P note any significant condition or finding about which nothing further appears to have been done?
- Review the physician's proposed plan of treatment. Are there documented care plans—medical and nursing?
- Does the intake documentation appear to be complete and accurate? Does any significant information appear to have been overlooked? Are there any blanks on any of the forms? What information is missing? Can it be determined why—are there any explanatory notes? Are all readily identifiable, obvious problems addressed?
- Who was the source of the information—the patient, a family member, other? What was his or her relationship to the patient?
- If it was someone other than the patient, why? Could this source be considered reliable? Were they authorized to act in lieu of the patient?
- Is there any evidence of the patient or family withholding information? Were they unable to provide it or did they refuse to provide it? What could such information be?
- If it was the patient, could his or her status or condition at that time have had any effect on the accuracy or reliability of the data they provided?
- Is there evidence of any degree of cognitive impairment?
- Is there any evidence of problems communicating—language, deafness? Was an interpreter utilized? Who was it? Were they qualified in this situation?
- Are the patient's allergies identified and properly noted?
- Does the list of the patient's valuables note such items as hearing aids, canes, glasses, prostheses?

Consent Forms

Routine Procedures

- Was the patient's consent expressed or implied?
- How is it documented? The record should contain a form that was signed by the patient or an authorized representative at the time of admission.
- Who requested and obtained it?
- By whom was it signed—the patient?
- What was the patient's status at that time—sedated, alert and oriented, in severe pain? Were they competent?
- If not signed by the patient, was it given by one who had the legal capacity to do so?
- By whom was it witnessed?
- When was the consent obtained? Coincident with admission?
- Were all questions answered and all significant points clarified?

Informed Consent

- Informed consent is required for any nonroutine diagnostic or therapeutic procedure, including invasive procedures such as surgery.
- Does the documentation show that all of the required elements of informed consent were present? These include:
  1. the patient, in giving his or her informed consent, fully comprehended the procedure, and all material risks;
  2. all material risks were disclosed, known to, or apparent to the patient and/or family;
  3. the expected therapeutic outcome was defined;
  4. untoward outcomes were also identified as far as possible;
  5. all significant adverse side effects and/or complications were presented;
  6. any alternative therapies, including none, were discussed;
  7. the information was provided and the consent obtained by the practitioner legally responsible for doing so; and

8. the patient was competent at the time of consent or, if not, the individual who gave consent was authorized to do so.

- If there appear to be any conflicting statements on the matter of informed consent, is it likely to be a health care provider's word against that of the plaintiff?

Transfer Records

- Was the patient transferred from another unit within the hospital or from an outside health care facility?
- What was the reason for the transfer? Was it routine?
- Did the medical records/chart accompany the patient?
- Who initiated the order for transfer?
- To what unit or facility was the patient transferred?
- What documentation indicates that it was necessary—what were the reasons, the rationale for it?
- At what time was it indicated as being necessary?
- At what time was the transfer protocol initiated?
- Was the transfer timely given the patient's status at that time?
- Does there appear to have been any undue delay in initiating it?
- At what time was the transfer procedure completed?
- How long did it take to complete the move—from transferring unit to receiving unit? Were there undue delays? If so, why?
- Was the patient's condition accurately communicated to the staff of the receiving facility or unit?
- Who gave the report on the patient's status?
- Who received the report?
- Was the patient properly stabilized prior to transfer?
- Was an adequate assessment done before, during, and afterward?
- Was there proper support staff, equipment, and mode of transportation during the transfer? Who and what were they? Are their notes included in the record?
- Was there a physician with the transport team, if required?
- Was there an RN with the transport team, if required?
- Were there any additions or changes to any medical records that may have remained at the transferring institution?

Providers' Progress Notes

Progress notes are a daily chronological narrative relating to the patient's diagnosis, course of treatment, response to the medical and nursing regimen, and the patient's ongoing status, up to and including discharge. It is here that the reviewer is most likely to find the answers to the critical questions.

Integrated progress notes include notes of physicians nurses and ancillary professionals, for example, physical, respiratory, and occupational therapists, social service, nutrition. These progress notes are usually integrated in a continuing chronological narrative.

What the reviewer is looking for may be in the nurses' notes, on one page out of several hundred in the record, or on one or two lines. Much of the rest of the record may be of no great use. Or, there may be nothing at all—no mention of the alleged incident. The incident and alleged injury that the plaintiff describes will likely be documented in an "Incident Report." This, it will be claimed by the defense, is nondiscoverable. Incident reports are discussed later in this chapter.

Focus on the *nurses' notes.* In a malpractice case, the examiner is strongly advised to focus on the significance of hospital charting from a *nursing* perspective and learn the language and formats of nurses' notes. Nursing records are a vital part of the patient's chart since nurses communicate and coordinate a patient's care with physicians as well as with the other departments of the hospital. Nurses' notes and their supplemental forms comprise a large portion of the medical records that will be reviewed and summarized, and they can provide some of the most significant and useful information. In cases of malpractice, nurses' notes can make or break a case. For an in-depth discussion of nursing documentation, the reader is referred to Sharpe 1999, chapter 9.

As the review proceeds, make a list of all medical, technical, or other unfamiliar terms. Prepare a glossary from this list and include this in the report. In reading the language of the medical record, do not assume that all medical, technical, scientific terms are being used correctly. Use a medical dictionary and check terms to be included in the glossary.

Progress notes will include those of medical and nursing staff in variety of units, services, and disciplines including:

- emergency rescue and transport,
- emergency department,
- surgery,
- coronary care,
- various intensive care units,

- radiology,
- dialysis,
- psychiatry,
- obstetrics, and
- neonatal.

In addition to the medical and nursing documentation, the notes of ancillary caregivers in special disciplines should be reviewed. These include:

- physical therapy,
- occupational therapy,
- respiratory therapy,
- nutritionists, and
- social and religious/spiritual services.

The progress notes, if any, of all providers involved in postdischarge treatment and rehabilitation should be obtained and reviewed. It must be determined if there has been patient compliance or noncompliance. The reviewer must confirm what was ordered, compliance with those orders, and the reasons for, and results of, noncompliance, if any. It will be necessary to determine if the patient:

- has attended all follow-up appointments for evaluation, treatment, and therapy;
- is adhering to any medication regimen;
- is following any dietary regimen;
- has changed his or her lifestyle as directed, that is, stopped smoking, using alcohol;
- is abiding by any restrictions on activities; and
- is following any exercise regimen prescribed.

General Review Questions and Points for Consideration in Progress Notes

There are a number of things the reviewer should be looking for in reading progress notes.

- Do physicians and nurses chart on separate progress notes or are their notes integrated (the usual format)?

- Is it evident that each group consulted and/or reviewed the appropriate records and notes of others to obtain a complete, accurate assessment of the patient's status?
- Is there any evidence that the nurses read the physicians' notes as required?
- Is there any evidence that the physicians read the nurses' notes as required?
- Do nurses' notes correlate to doctors' progress notes and vice versa?
- Do nurses notes compare with those of other staff? Are there any apparent contradictions or conflicts among providers?
- Are there any personal comments, characterizations, or derogatory statements about other staff?
- Do any staff notes infer or assign blame, attempt to settle personal conflicts, criticize, or accuse? Is there any indication of a "chart war"?
- Were all actual or potential problems noted as having been reported to the appropriate physician or to a nursing supervisor? Is this documented fully—no "doctor notified" statements?
- Are there any statements to the effect that a provider "informed" a colleague? Is there evidence that such an individual was *fully* informed?
- Do all statements in the notes conform to those in the discovery documents? This will be a primary focus.
- Are there any statements anywhere in the notes indicating liability?
- Are there any attempts to explain or rationalize mistakes? Note the use of such words as "accident," "accidentally," "somehow."
- Are the nurses' assessments, opinions, or conclusions based on the supporting data presented in the medical records? Nurses' notes should not contain assumptions, opinions, or unfounded conclusions. They should be completely objective. There should be no "appears to be," "seems to be," and other such statements. Any subjective comments must be supported by documented facts.
- Are all notes FACT? That is: Factual, Accurate, Complete, Timely.
- Are all commentaries in the notes appropriate? Is there any "labeling" of the patient? Are there any derogatory remarks about the patient or his or her family?

- Are there quotes where appropriate? Any paraphrasing? Who is being paraphrased?
- *Are there any secrets*? Is anyone trying to hide something?
- Do all the facts speak for themselves?
- Are the facts being down-played? Does the record speak for itself?
- Are all data, facts, and times consistent throughout the record? This is a critical element.
- Does the documentation reflect continuity and consistency of care?
- Is there any evidence of:
    1. Failure to properly monitor the patient—to continuously evaluate and reevaluate the patient—failure to provide continuity of care?
    2. Failure to identify those signs and symptoms requiring notification of physician?
    3. Failure to report and communicate promptly changes in status?
    4. Failure to follow up and/or clarify?
    5. Failure to proceed up the chain of command?
    6. Failure to report errors promptly?
    7. Failure to report the incompetency or impairment of others?
    8. Failure to provide for patient safety?
    9. Failure to intervene in a timely and appropriate manner?
    10. Failure to check and monitor all equipment in use? Did any products or equipment have specific instructions for use? Were these read? Were they followed?
- Was there any computerized charting of any progress notes? In what media were they preserved? Are they included in the medical record?

General Format and Language of Progress Notes

If a reviewer can acquire a basic understanding of the principles and formats of charting and common medical terms and abbreviations, he or she can effectively analyze any medical record. Charting formats vary according to facility and practitioner. Frequently both physicians and nurses will use a format referred to as "SOAP":

Subjective: derived from the patient's statements—symptoms

Objective: observations of signs or other presenting factors

Assessment: interpretation and summary of findings, "rule out" statements

Plan: of treatment, management of care

Examining Progress Notes

In reading the progress notes, there are a number of specific questions to ask.

- Is all language clear or is it vague, general, ambiguous, or self-serving?
- Are the uses of medical terms and abbreviations correct and consistent?
- Do the notes communicate significant, meaningful information or are they filled with trivia?
- Does all documentation conform to the requirements of the facility's P&P?
- What format and forms are used for progress notes? Are these used consistently by all staff?
- Are there any notes, charting, or records that are not on the forms required by the facility? Why not?
- Was summary charting done or were events charted as they occurred?
- Is "charting by exception" approved and defined in the P&P manual?
- Is presumption of "not charted not done" in favor of nurse?
- According to the P&P, what staff are permitted to chart?
- Was all charting done by the appropriate staff—that is, authorized staff?
- Was charting done on each shift—regardless of patient's status?
- Is every note dated? Do all dates follow P&P format, for example, military time?
- Do all times agree? This is a critical point. Times must be consistent throughout the record.
- Is every note signed? Are all signatures in accordance with P&P?
- Are all notes requiring countersignatures countersigned as required by P&P?
- Does the countersigner indicate that the entry was reviewed and the content approved?

- Is there any indication of notes written by one person and signed by another?
- Was the individual who wrote the notes the one who actually provided the care or performed the procedures described?
- Are there any significant changes in any notes? Are the reasons for such changes properly documented?
- Have any previously written notes been altered in any way?
- Is there any evidence that anyone was pressured to alter any entries?
- Does each page of the nurses' notes and all other documents have the patient's name stamped on it with the addressograph plate? Pages with such information written in might be suspect as having been prepared at a later date and inserted into the record.
- Which, if any, documents are not stamped? Are these critical?
- Is there an excessive number of blank spaces, lines, or pages? This is not acceptable in that is allows for "sanitization" of a record.
- Are there any gaps in the record, that is, long intervals passing when it appears that nothing has transpired in patient care? This could be evidence of "abandonment," or failure to properly and timely monitor and assess a patient.
- Do any individual pages or sections of the record appear to be missing?
- Is there any evidence of notes or pages having been recopied? Note particularly any photocopied pages on which newly written notes have been inserted in any section.
- Were all original copies retained and all pages identified as such? Photocopying a document is acceptable provided that the original document is retained.
- Are all documents legible or is the handwriting of certain individuals consistently sloppy or unreadable?
- Do the notes reflect use of proper grammar, syntax, spelling, and punctuation?

Errors in Documentation

- Does there seem to be a pattern? Do certain individuals make frequent, consistent errors?
- How are errors indicated? The most acceptable way is to draw a single line through the incorrect entry and write the correct information *next to it* on the same line. An entry written above the

corrected one does not confirm when it was written—at that moment, or sometime afterward?

- How are errors corrected? There should be no erasures or "white out." If either are evident in the copy, examine the original. If a liquid correction fluid has been used, the original document may have to be X-rayed to reveal what has been obliterated.
- Is the manner of correction consistent for each individual?
- Does the manner of correction conform to P&P?
- Are all corrected errors still legible? If not, examine the original.
- Is there any evidence of early entries, i.e. charting done before the fact?
- Is there any evidence of late entries, i.e. charting done long after the fact? All entries are made after the fact, but should be done as soon after the events as possible. There are a number of questions to ask.
  1. By whom were the late entries made?
  2. Is there a pattern evident?
  3. Why were they necessary?
  4. Are all late entries clearly identified as such? How?
  5. Is the date and time of the event documented accurately?
  6. Is there any evidence of backdating of entries?
  7. Are all late entries cross-referenced to the proper page and place?
  8. Are any significant omissions of notes charted as new entries?
  9. Does any late entry describe the events surrounding the incident of alleged malpractice and injury? *These bear particular scrutiny*!!

Abbreviations or Symbols

Note and define all abbreviations, especially those that could have more than one meaning or interpretation (e.g., SOB—short of breath). (See appendix IV.) Include each abbreviation in the glossary. An entire case can turn on the meaning, interpretation, or correctness of an abbreviation. In that situation, it may be necessary to obtain the list of the hospital's approved abbreviations as shown in their policy and procedure manual *at the time of the incident*.

Medical report abbreviations are somewhat standardized. However, each institution or each form may use individualized representations. Some reports use abbreviations or codes that may not be found in a regular dictionary or in a medical dictionary. The source's medical records department may have to be contacted to obtain the code key list or other guide to these entries. Professional organizations often utilize uniform abbreviations or code guides. Regardless of standards, lists, or dictionaries, practitioners frequently improvise abbreviations. Generally, however, there is consistency in use of case and punctuation. When an abbreviation is encountered, ask:

- Are all abbreviations used throughout the records consistent with the P&P manual list of approved abbreviations;
- was there such a list in effect at the time of the incident? Obtain the list *in effect at the time of the incident;*
- are all abbreviations used consistently by all staff; and
- are there any abbreviations that could have been or were misinterpreted?

These will be critical considerations if the alleged injury could have been the result of an improperly written or misinterpreted abbreviation.

Flow Sheets, Patient Care Check Lists, Graphic Charts

- In which units were flow sheets used?
- Do they indicate routine check-off or a routine duplication of previous shifts check-offs?
- Do the progress notes verify the information noted on the flowsheets completely and accurately—and conversely?
- Are there any significant discrepancies between flowsheets and progress notes? What are the inconsistencies?
- Are significant deviations or exceptions charted in the notes and flagged on the flowsheet?
- Does the vital sign graphic chart show any significant deviation from normal parameters?
- Is there evidence that appropriate communication and intervention was initiated on the basis of these data?

Nursing Care Plans

In the past, nursing care plans were often discarded when the patient was discharged.

- What was the facility's policy regarding the use and format of care plans?

- Were care plans preprinted or computer generated or prepared individually?
- Was there an individualized care plan in the medical record for the patient?
- Is the care plan complete?
- Was this care plan in place at the time of the alleged event?
- Is there any indication that all nurses involved read and utilized the plan?
- Do all nurses' notes reflect conformity with the care plan?
- Could the care plan be relevant to the alleged incident?

Nursing Diagnoses

Nursing care plans usually include nursing "orders" based on nursing "diagnoses"—an arguably pseudoscientific approach. Nursing diagnoses are usually convoluted restatements of physicians' orders and/or diagnoses. In reviewing nursing care plans, if any are included in the record, the reader may note a number of nursing diagnoses. He or she should consider the significance of these from the aspect of patient care and legal implications.

Nursing diagnoses are defined as those health problems that have the potential for resolution by means of nursing actions. Patients' nursing problems are defined in terms of a nursing diagnoses. They are *not* medical diagnoses, medical treatments, or diagnostic studies. They are *not* the problems that a nurse experiences while delivering patient care. They are clinical judgments of those problems that have the "*potential*" to be resolved by means of nursing intervention.

From a legal aspect, many nurse practice acts do not address the matter of nurses making such diagnoses. Those that do often fail to define what the term means. For example, the Pennsylvania Nurse Practice Act defines the practice of professional nursing as : "diagnosing and treating human responses to actual or potential health problems. . . . [The] foregoing shall not be deemed to include acts of medical diagnosis or prescription of medical therapy."

From the perspective of many in the nursing profession, nursing diagnoses have been described as: redundant terminology that clouds communication; as statements of the obvious; and as so much doublespeak to describe medical clinical symptoms and diagnoses. Anything is acceptable as long as it is not used by physicians. This is perceived by many nurses as creating pretentious barriers with others in the health care profession and as just another way to confuse the patient (Sharpe 1999, chapter 8).

Delegation of Care

By Nurses

- Is there any indication of care having been delegated? By whom? To whom—UAP, LPN, NA, other?
- Was such delegation appropriate given the circumstances?
- What was the P&P of the facility regarding delegation of care?
- Were any family members or other visitors allowed to assist in the patient's care or supervision?
- What was the extent of such participation or assistance?
- Was such participation appropriate given the circumstances?
- Was it approved, directed, supervised, or taught by a nurse?
- What is the policy of the facility regarding such participation in care?

By a Physician Assistant (PA) or Physician Extender (PE)

A physician who employs or collaborates with a PA or PE is liable for any negligence on the part of such an individual. The physician is also liable for any nonmedical actions by such a person if the physician is found negligent in screening or supervision. The review should identify any procedures that were carried out by a PA or any orders that may have been given by such a practitioner. There are a number of questions to be considered; many of these will not be answerable from the medical record and may have to be pursued in other sources.

- Were such actions in compliance the institution's policies and procedures?
- Were there written protocols in place? Did these clearly define:
    1. the PA's scope of practice;
    2. actions that the PA could initiate independently;
    3. actions that required consultation with a physician;
    4. the type of patient and/or degree of acuity that the PA could treat?
- Were any acts of medical diagnosis and/or treatment specifically delegated in writing?
- What are the provisions of state statutes regarding the licensing and scope of practice of such practitioners?
- Were the PA's actions within the scope of state law?

- Were the actions within their scope of practice as defined in the statutes?
- Did the practitioner have a current, valid state license?
- Did the PA have the education, training, and experience required?
- Was there adequate supervision by a physician? Does the record confirm that a physician was fully aware of all actions taken by the assistant? Were all PA orders countersigned by a physician as required?

Student Nurses' Notes

- Was any care given by a student nurse?
- Are the student's notes complete and consistent with those of the staff nurses'?
- Who was the student's coassigned nurse?
- What was the policy of the facility and/or the educational institution regarding student nurses' notes being countersigned by a clinical instructor or coassigned staff nurse?
- Were student nurses' notes countersigned?
- Do student nurses' care or progress notes have any relevancy to the alleged incident?

Scope of Practice—Deviations

- Is there any evidence that any health care provider acted outside of their scope of practice?
- Is there any evidence of a nurse making a medical diagnosis?
- Are there any actions by a nurse that were done without a physician's order where such an order is required?
- Is there any evidence that the nurse negligently performed a procedure that was not required or ordered?
- Is there any evidence that the nurse performed a procedure that caused injury?
- Is there any evidence that a nurse or any other individual assumed or performed duties that were not commensurate with their educational preparation, training, and documented proficiency?
- Are there any actions *not* documented that would be considered the nurse's "usual practice" under the circumstances?

- Is there documentation of any care or procedures that were *not* done? What are the reasons? Are they valid?
- Is there any evidence that nurses were ordered or pressured to deviate in any way from the standards of care? By whom?

Procedures

- Who ordered the procedure(s)?
- What were the procedures?
- Who carried out or participated in the procedure?
- Was there any undue delay in starting a procedure? What was the duration? Why?
- Is there any evidence of a procedure being interrupted? Why was the procedure interrupted? How long was the interruption?
- Did any procedure(s) take a longer than normal time to complete? Why?
- Are there any indications of offers of assistance? Was such needed? Who offered, accepted, declined—why?
- Was the procedure documented completely, including the outcome and patient response?

Surgical Procedures and Reports

- Review all preoperative findings and diagnoses to confirm the rationale and need for surgery.
- Study all operating room notes—surgeons' and nurses'—to identify any untoward events or "surgical misadventures."
- Identify each of the surgeons participating and the status of each, that is, who was in charge—who was "captain of the ship"?
- Prepare a summary description of the surgical procedure in lay terms.
- Identify the anesthesiologist and the type and route of anesthesia. Review the anesthesiologist's notes for any unusual events.
- Review all recovery room (PACU) notes to determine the patient's postoperative status and tolerance of the procedure.
- Review the documentation of all postoperative findings by medical and nursing staff.
- Note if any specimens were removed for biopsy or testing and review the results of such tests if they might be relevant.

- Prepare a summary postoperative report, including findings, diagnosis, prognosis.

Patient Safety

- Are all appropriate and necessary interventions for patient safety documented?
- Are there any interventions for patient safety that were indicated and that were not implemented or documented?
- What was the P&P regarding restraints? Were there written orders or protocols?
- If restraints were used, were they ordered by a physician?
- If restraints were initiated by the nurse, were they medically necessary?
- Is the need for restraints fully documented?
- Is the patient's response to and tolerance of restraints fully documented?
- Is there any evidence that the patient could have been injured by the method of application or by the device itself?
- If the alleged injury was the result of a fall, note from the medication administration record if the patient had been given any medications just prior that could have impaired the patient's faculties. Should the side rails of the bed have been raised after that medication was given?

Patient Behaviors and Responses

- What was the patient's status at the time of the alleged incident—conscious, alert and oriented, lethargic, sedated, comatose?
- Is the documentation of the patient's response to care, interventions, therapies, and other provider contacts complete and accurate?
- Does documentation indicate:
    1. any openly hostile statements about the staff, the institution, or the course of treatment;
    2. persistent criticism of the staff, the treatment, the food;
    3. unwarranted overreactions to any events;
    4. refusal to accept any responsibility for their own care?

- Are there any indications that a patient refused a medication, treatment, or procedure? (With few exceptions, that is the patient's right.)
- Is any noncompliant behavior of the patient fully documented?
- Is there any noncompliant behavior by family members or visitors noted?
- Is the patient's or family's behavior described objectively?
- Could any patient and/or family noncompliance have contributed to the alleged injury?
- Was any contraband found at any time? What was it? Who provided it? Could it have been a contributing factor?
- Is the patient quoted exactly or paraphrased regarding self-assessments?
- Are there any personal comments, characterizations, or derogatory statements about patient or the family? Are there any "labels" applied?
- Do any provider notes reflect any insensitivity to patient complaints?
- Were legitimate patient complaints taken seriously?
- Was there a failure to address the patients emotional and psychosocial needs as well as physical/medical needs?
- Does any provider appear to have been authoritarian, inflexible, or intolerant in attitude or behavior?
- Are patient or family questions and concerns documented? Are staff responses to these documented?
- Is there documentation of appropriate teaching and assessment of understanding—during time of admission, throughout the period of hospitalization, and at time of discharge?
- Is there any evidence that the patient requested a review of and/or a copy of his or her medical record at any time during the hospitalization? Was this done? Who was present?
- Can it be determined from the patient's statements in the record if he or she has initiated previous malpractice suits?
  1. What was the nature of these suits?
  2. What was the outcome of these suits?
  3. Could this person be a malingerer—a professional litigant, a professional patient?

Physicians' Orders

These are written or verbal directives to nursing and ancillary services and to other physicians regarding all medications and treatments. Their purpose is to communicate the plan of medical care to all other members of the health care team. These orders include: (1) preadmission, (2) admission, (3) ongoing, (4) preoperative, (5) postoperative, and (6) discharge.

Where a question of an order is at issue, ask:

- Who gave the order(s)—a staff physician, intern, resident, physician's assistant?
- Was the order in question written or oral?
- Exactly how was it phrased?
- Does it appear to be complete? Were there any omissions?
- Was the order clear and unambiguous?

Verbal Orders

- Was the physician physically present when an order was given?
- Were there any telephone orders? Were these documented as having been read back to the physician and confirmed by him or her as correct?
- Who took any verbal orders—an RN?
- Are all verbal orders countersigned by the originating physician? What was the P&P regarding countersigning?
- Was this done in accordance with the P&P? Were all verbal orders countersigned within the prescribed time?

Written Orders

- Was there a physician's order in all cases where such was required?
- Is the date and time of each order noted? This is a must!
- Is every written order legible?
- Was each order transcribed exactly as written?
- Were there any apparent transcription errors?
- By whom was the order transcribed—by an RN, unit assistant/clerk?
- Was the transcriber authorized to do so?
- What was the date and time the order was transcribed? Was there any undue delay? Why?

- By whom was the transcribed order checked? What was the date, time? Was there any undue delay? Why?
- What was the P&P regarding illegible, incomplete, or inaccurate orders? Was it followed?
- Were any incorrect or questionable orders questioned and clarified? How was this documented?
- Is there any documentation of efforts to contact the physician to clarify an order? If not successful what further action, if any, was taken?
- If the staff were not able to reach the physician, why not?
- Were all new orders compatible with old orders if appropriate? Were there any significant changes? Are the reasons documented?
- What was the timing of the implementation of new orders? Were they effected within a reasonable time?
- Were "stat" orders carried out *immediately*?

Standing Orders

- Were there any standing orders or written protocols?
- What were they?
- On what dates were they originally established?
- Were all parameters for implementation clearly defined?
- Were all standing orders executed by the staff properly signed and countersigned?
- When were any standing orders executed by the staff?
- Was there an expiration date indicated? Was this exceeded?
- Is there documented rationale for each standing order executed?
- Were there any standing orders stating such as "renew all previous orders"?
- Were all such orders in compliance with P&P?
- Did the physician communicate all necessary information about the patient's history, diagnosis, prognosis?
- Was there a DNR or "no code" order? Was this order *written* by a physician?

Medications and the Medication Administration Record (MAR)

When listing medications, include the purpose of each medication and any significant side effects. Include these in your report. If the alleged injury is claimed to be the result of an error in medication administration, ask:

- Who administered the medication—RN, LPN, student nurse?
- Is there any indication that any medications involved were ones that the physician or nurse might not have administered previously or may not have been familiar with?
- Were there specific instructions for preparation and administration included, for example, package inserts, pharmacy sheets,? Did the physician or nurse read the information and instructions?
- Were any other references checked prior to giving the drugs? What references were checked? Were these authoritative? Was the pharmacy consulted? Who responded?
- Were the frequency and/or intervals of pain medication administration appropriate?
- Does the record of administration of medications for pain reflect appropriate pain management and intervention by the staff?
- Were there any apparent undue delays in administering pain medications?
- Were the medications, routes, and doses appropriate based on the patient's complaints and the provider's assessment of the patient's pain?
- Were all premedication assessments fully documented?
- Were any and all allergies fully documented, noted, and confirmed prior to administration of medications?
- Was the patient advised of risks and adverse side effects when appropriate?
- Were there any indications that the patient refused a medication? Were the reasons fully documented? Is the patient quoted? Was a physician advised? What were his or her instructions?
- Were the patient's responses to *all* medications fully documented?
- Is there an MAR for each day of hospitalization?
- Are all MARs complete regarding dates, times, routes, doses?
- Are all medications given properly signed off?

- Do all initials in signed off medications match those with signature?
- Were there any standing orders (PRN orders)?
- Were all standing orders signed off, countersigned?
- Was there complete documentation for any medications given under standing orders—justification, assessment parameters, or other circumstances?
- Were all doses ordered in the unit of measure in which they were dispensed?
- Was the dose given appropriate to the patient's documented weight?
- What system was used—apothecary or metric?
- Was a "unit-dose" system in place?
- Were any generic medications given?
- Were all generic medications approved and/or ordered by a physician?
- Were any substitutions made without a physician's order or knowledge?
- Was the generic medication one that is used regularly in the unit?
- Were all medications ordered listed in the facility's drug formulary at that time?

Preprinted Order Forms for Medications

- Were any preprinted pharmacy order forms used?
- Was the form used developed by a physician, pharmacy, or provided by an outside source—for example, drug company?
- Did each form have an identification number printed on it?
- Did the form comply with P&P?
- Does the form use proper drug nomenclature?
- Is the form free of confusing abbreviations, misspellings, and other errors?
- Are there any unapproved abbreviations, symbols, or terminology?
- Do all copies match the original?
- Does the form comply with JCAHO, state, or other regulatory body's rules and regulations?

- Does the form require nurses to perform any duties outside their scope of practice?
- Was the form filled out properly and completely and in accordance with P&P?

MAR

- Was the MAR computer generated or handwritten?
- Who prepared it—pharmacy, RN, unit clerk?
- Was it checked for accuracy by an RN?

Medications

- Were the six "rights" of medication administration observed? The right:
  1. patient,
  2. time,
  3. medication,
  4. dose,
  5. route, and
  6. technique?
- Were any medications contraindicated for any reason? Were the reasons documented?
- Are there any consistent patterns evident regarding medication errors—times, drugs, patient, dosage, doses missed?
- How were these events documented? Was this in conformity with P&P?
- Were any medications missed? If so, why?
- Is there a pattern of medication omissions?
- How are missed medications documented on the MAR? A circle drawn around a time/initials entry usually indicates that a medication was missed.
- How are missed medications documented in the nurse's notes? Are the reasons for medications not having been given stated? Are they valid reasons?
- Was the patient's response to an omitted medication documented?
- Were any medications administered early or late?
- Is there a pattern of medications being given early or late?

- Are the reasons documented? Are they valid?
- How are they documented in the nurse's notes?
- Was the patient's response to a medication given early or late documented?
- Note any frequent changes in times in the schedule of administration of medications. This may be an indication of staff failure in administration routine and scheduling. Are the reasons for changes in the schedule documented?
- Does the schedule of administration confirm to the physician's order?
- Did all medications (e.g., narcotics) that required an expiration date on an order have that date indicated on the MAR? Were any given after that expiration date?

Parenteral (IV) Medications

- Does documentation include:
    1. the time the IV line was inserted,
    2. the initial and any subsequent sites,
    3. frequency of site checks,
    4. the size and type of the needle,
    5. the time the IV flow was started,
    6. the type of solution used initially,
    7. any additives to the solution?
- Who inserted the IV line? Was it an RN or a phlebotomist?
- Were any problems noted?
- How many attempts were made? By whom?
- Was the individual who inserted the IV certified?
- Who set up the solution bag, tubing, pump? What types were used?
- Who prepared any medication or other additive and placed in the bag—an RN, pharmacy staff?
- What was the date and time it was prepared?
- How soon after that date and time was it delivered to the unit and started?
- What was the medication—name, type, dose? Was it as ordered?
- What was the type and amount of solution it was placed in? Was it the solution ordered? Was it the in the volume ordered?

- Was administration by pump (type?) or gravity flow?
- What was the rate of infusion ordered? Was the correct rate of infusion shown by the IV flow sheets? Calculate and confirm.
- Was the total amount of fluid volume infused as ordered? Was there any excess of deficiency? Calculate and confirm.
- Who started the infusion?
- Who monitored and recorded the infusion?
- Is the infusion flowsheet correct? Were the correct amounts infused over the prescribed times? Calculate and confirm.
- Was the infusion interrupted for any significant period of time? Why?
- Do the progress notes confirm that the IV site was monitored and changed according to P&P?
- Is there any notation regarding infiltration at the insertion site?
- Were there any injuries to tissues as a result of extravasation of an IV solution?
- Is there any indication of infection at a site?

Reports of Other Diagnostic Tests and Procedures

These will include:(1) laboratory reports; (2) pathology reports; (3) radiology/nuclear medicine reports such as X-ray, CAT, and MRI; (4) any other studies including EEG, and EKG.

- Is there any indication that the appropriate staff failed to perform any proper, indicated, or ordered lab tests or other diagnostic studies?
- Was there any evidence of a failure to request proper lab tests and diagnostic studies where such were indicated as being necessary?
- Could these be tests that any physician or nurse would know should have been done?
- Do time and date stamps on lab slips reflect proper implementation of physicians' orders?
- Do all lab tests support the treatment plan? Do they appear to have been appropriate given the patient's diagnosis?
- Could there be an excessive number of unwarranted tests?
- How were lab results reported—computer printout, hand delivered to unit, telephone?

- What time period was involved—start to finish?
- Did nurses properly interpret and act upon lab reports and diagnostic results?
- Did nurses follow up on lab reports and data? How was this documented?
- Do nurses' notes reflect physicians' being advised of lab reports? Was such notice timely? How was the physician notified?
- Do nurses' notes reflect physicians' follow up and new orders?

Consultation Reports

- Were consults ordered?
- Are all consults documented completely?
- Why was a consult ordered?
- By whom were consults ordered?
- Who were the consultants?
- What was the clinical specialty of each consultant?
- Was there timely initiation of a consult order and reporting of the results?
- What were the findings of the report and were these significant in the patient's claim?
- Does the report support the treating physicians' findings and plan of care?
- Were any recommendations of consultants implemented? If not, why not?
- Could there be any consult reports considered privileged?
- Were any postdischarge consults ordered? Are these reports in the medical record?

Discharge Documentation

Virtually every hospital requires that, at the time a patient is released from treatment, a discharge summary be prepared. This is done by both a physician and, usually, also by a member of the nursing staff. Although their respective format and content may differ, their summaries should be a complete, accurate recounting of all significant medical and nursing care and treatment during the patient's hospital stay. The physician's discharge summary should include:

1. an evaluation of the patient's response to treatment;
2. a confirmation of the physicians' final diagnosis;
3. a outline of the postdischarge plan, including a follow-up care regimen;
4. a statement of the patient's condition at time of discharge; and
5. full documentation of the discharge instructions given to the patient and/or their family.

Ask:

- Was a discharge summary prepared?
- Who prepared it?
- Is the physician's and/or nursing summary in the record?
- When was it prepared? Was its preparation timely with the discharge?
- If it was dictated, how long after the date of discharge was it transcribed?
- Does the discharge summary reflect all pertinent data contained in the progress notes?
- Does it correctly and completely summarize all care provided?
- Are there any significant details, findings, or comments in it that were not previously noted elsewhere in the medical record?
- Does it meet the documentation requirements of JCAHO, especially regarding discharge teaching?
- Does it describe all teaching and materials provided at discharge?
- Is the alleged incident of malpractice described or alluded to?

The reviewer should endeavor to answer several additional questions from the discharge summary.

- Is there any indication of premature discharge?
- Who was involved in the patient's discharge—staff, family members, others?
- Are all discharge instructions fully documented?
- Who received the discharge instructions?
- Is the content of the discharge instructions and plan fully documented? By whom?
- What did the teaching consist of? Were written instructions such

as brochures or handouts provided or were there verbal instructions only?

- How was the patient's or family's understanding of the material demonstrated? Was this documented?
- Who accompanied the patient from the facility at time of discharge?
- How did the patient leave the unit—ambulatory, WC, litter?
- What was the patient's cognitive status at the time?

The Discharge Summary and the Hearsay Rule

The hearsay rule, which was discussed in chapter 3, requires that any entry in a record be made by an individual who has personal knowledge of the event that he or she is recording or that the information was provided directly to the person making the entry by someone who had such personal knowledge.

This may be problematical in the writing of a discharge summary. If the physician (or nurse) charged with preparing it had not personally cared for a patient on an ongoing basis, it could be argued that the discharge summary they prepared does not satisfy the personal knowledge requirement. As patient care assignments can change frequently for both physicians and nurses, a practitioner may have had only casual, transient contact with a patient prior to having written the discharge summary. There may have been no opportunity to acquire personal knowledge of the subject.

In reviewing the patient's history and other data in the record and summarizing these, the physician acquires personal knowledge of the *data only*. Problems can arise, however, if the practitioner draws unfounded conclusions about the patient's status or prognosis at the time of discharge based solely on the information that others have provided in the record and not on personal knowledge and/or direct care of the *patient*. This failure could be legal grounds for attacking the admissibility of such conclusions at trial. The medical records reviewer must confirm that the individual who prepared the discharge summary meets the personal knowledge requirement.

Autopsy Report

An autopsy report is essential in a claim of wrongful death. Did the patient's family request an autopsy? Was an autopsy done? Is the report included in the medical record? The reviewer may have to obtain the report from a medical examiner or coroner. Note the findings of the autopsy regarding the cause of death. Are these consistent with any such statements in the medical record? Determine exactly who made the declaration of death. (In some states nurses are permitted by law to do so.)

PATIENT CONFIDENTIALITY

- Does it appear that patient confidentiality was maintained at all times?
- Was any information disclosed without the patient's consent?
- Is there any indication that any staff member improperly disclosed excessive or inappropriate information?
- Was the patient's status discussed with any unauthorized persons?
- Was any information given over the telephone in response to an inappropriate query?
- Are any other patients referred to by their names?

ADDITIONAL RECORDS THAT MAY REQUIRE REVIEW

As the review of documents contained in the medical record proceeds, there may be any number of additional questions, points, or references derived that may require obtaining, reviewing, and analyzing a variety of additional records that might contain information relevant to the issues.

Miscellaneous Facility or Provider Records

- Ambulance crew/EMT notes. These could be a source of witnesses. They will provide a summary of the patient's status prior to admission at the emergency room. Determine if any photographs or videos were taken by police, rescue personnel, or observers at the scene.
- Physicians' or clinic office records
- Correspondence—between patient and physician
- Itemized billing statements
- Referrals
- Quality Assurance Department records for any reports and/or recommendations relevant to the alleged incident, or past problems
- Risk Management Department records

- Relevant committee records and minutes of meetings—if these are accessible or discoverable
- Any relevant JCAHO accreditation and review reports prepared following the date of the alleged incident. Note particularly any JCAHO comments regarding departments, units, or personnel who may be involved in the incident.
- Relevant reports of government agencies—local, state, federal
- Reports of the Infection Control Department, if relevant
- Reports from plant engineering, and maintenance. Note any similar prior events, and incidents.
- Purchasing department records of returns of defective equipment, material, or supplies (The manufacturers of equipment and supplies may have to be contacted to determine incidents of previous problems and any resulting lawsuits.)
- Central Supply Department records of defective materials complaints, and previous problems reported
- Pharmacy records of problems with particular medications
- Biomedical engineering department reports of repairs or records of failure of equipment that was involved in the alleged incident. Is there a pattern evident?

Policies and Procedures

- What were the relevant policies and procedures in effect *at the time* of the incident?
- Are these still in effect at the present time?
- What revisions were made since that time?
- When were they made relative to the date of the incident?
- Are the revisions in any way relevant to the alleged incident?
- When was the last time the staff member(s) involved in the incident reviewed the P&P?

Nursing Administration Records

- Is there any evidence that supervisors or managers were aware that the nurse was not trained or competent in a given task or assignment?
- Is there any evidence that supervisors or managers made assignments that were beyond the training or abilities of the nurse?

- Was the charge nurse or nurse manager aware of any previous similar incidents involving the same staff member?
- Are there any acts or omissions by supervisors or managers that may have contributed to the incident?
- Is there any indication that supervisors or managers provided erroneous instructions or directives?
- Are there any references to staffing problems and reporting or resolution of such problems? How were these reported? How were they resolved? By whom?
- What was the nursing staffing situation on the unit at the time of the incident? Is there any indication that patient-to-staff ratios were excessive to a degree to possibly compromise patient care?
- What was the nurse-patient ratio for the nurse-defendant at the time of the event?
- What was the level of acuity of each patient assigned to the nurse?
- Were the nurses or other staff involved in the incident working a regular eight-hour shift, a twelve-hour shift, a double shift? How long were individual staff on duty?
- At what time did the incident occur? (Statistics show that the largest number of patient care errors occur between 0300 and 0600.)
- What was the patient care model used on the unit involved? Was it team nursing, primary nursing, or another model?
- Was the nurse involved regularly assigned to the unit or was he or she a "float" nurse?
- If the nurse was a float nurse, is it documented that he or she was trained and qualified to work on the particular unit?
- What was the frequency of previous assignments to that unit, if any?
- Were they any admissions coincident with the event? What did these involve—acuity of patient, stat orders, procedures? Was the unit particularly busy at the time of the incident?
- Were any admissions assigned to the nurse involved in the incident?
- How many admissions did the nurse(s) involved in the incident have during the course of that shift?
- Was additional staffing provided to handle such admissions? Were requests for such assistance documented?

- Was the nurse involved in the incident employed by the facility or was he or she an agency nurse?
- As an agency nurse, did he or she have any past assignments in the institution or the particular unit? How many? The agency records may have to be obtained and reviewed for any prior complaints or incidents.
- Could a unit clerk/secretary/assistant be involved in any way—as a witness or as a possible defendant? Confirm his or her role at the time of the incident and any possible liability. Could he or she have transcribed a physician's order incorrectly?

Personnel and Employment History Records

- Do the personnel files include complete resumes?
- Was all information on the employment application checked and verified?
- Were references checked? Employment records from previous employers might be obtained and reviewed for any relevancy.
- Does the file contain any prior complaints against the staff involved in the alleged incident?
- What was the nature of these complaints?
- Are there any prior disciplinary actions against the staff member?
- Had the practitioner been licensed and/or practiced in any other state or country?
- Does the personnel file or resume show any unusual pattern of frequent interstate/intrastate relocation and job changes? Pay particular attention to prior employment in another state(s). Ask why these interstate moves were made.
- Is there any history of frequent terminations? Why?
- What are the details—dates, places, reasons?
- Could there be any personal history that might be part of the public record?
- Could there be any prior criminal or civil suits against the defendant?
- Has the defendant ever been the subject of proceedings by a state licensing board?
- Who filed the complaint?
- What was the outcome of the proceedings—suspension, revocation, probation, other?

- What are the practitioner's professional association affiliations?
- What is the educational level of the practitioner involved in the incident?
- What is the educational background of the practitioner—names of institutions, dates attended, dates graduated, degrees? GPA, honors, student activities?
- Is the practitioner certified in any specialty area? What was the certifying organization? What was the certification procedure, and qualifications? When was the certification effective? Is the certification documented as current?
- If a nurse is/was an advanced practice nurse (APN), was he or she functioning as such at the time and in a unit or site of such specialty?
- What was the scope, content, and duration of orientation of the practitioner at time of hire?
- Were all of their clinical skills current and documented as such? This would include documentation of inservices, seminars, CEUs.
- Was the practitioner properly trained and experienced in the particular procedure involved in the incident? Is this documented?
- What were the job descriptions of all staff members involved in incident?
- Did any of the nurses involved have clinical privileges? What was the extent of these? When were they granted? When were they last reviewed?
- Was the National Practitioner Data Bank (NPDB) queried prior to granting clinical privileges to any new staff as required by law?
- Is there an *original* copy of the practitioner's professional license in the file? Is the license current? Was it current at the time of the incident?

INCIDENT REPORTS

"An incident report is a written description, factual and nonjudgmental, of an event that caused an injury (or had the potential to cause and injury). It doesn't belong in the patient's medical record, nor does any mention that it's been filled out" (Cournoyer 1995, 21). Virtually all such reports are prepared by staff nurses and reviewed and signed by an attending physician and a nursing supervisor. The incident report, the "unusual occurrence" report, is the place where "untoward" events are documented—it should be the *only* place.

An untoward or extraordinary event is one that is defined as a *marked deviation* from the normal clinical routine. Any such event usually requires the preparation of an incident report *whether or not a patient or anyone else has been any injured.* A report should detail the circumstances of an event that caused an injury or those factors *predictive* of a possible injury. The deviation from the routine may be any situation that is considered inconsistent with the institution's normal operation or with the care of patients in any clinical setting. This would always include any incident which could possibly result in a charge of liability on the part of the institution.

Incident reports are virtually always prepared by the nursing staff. The preferred and widely used format is a check list arranged by a number of categories such as time, place, patient's condition, nature of injury if any, and staff involved. There will be a very limited space for comments; this precludes any subjective narrative description of the circumstances of the event that could be problematic. As a general rule, only *one* copy is prepared. Staff are advised that the report should present *facts only,* and that any subjective comments or statements should not be included. The report must not include any conclusions, assumptions, or opinions. There should be no unfounded statements of any kind. There should *never* be any language that admits liability or that might convey any suggestion of fault or blame. *And there must be no reference to the incident report anywhere in the chart.*

Purpose of the Incident Report

To maintain their JCAHO accreditation, a health care institution is required to set up and maintain an incident reporting system that complies with JCAHO standards and guidelines. The system functions as part of the risk management and quality assurance programs of the institution; the primary purpose is to provide an effective means to review and evaluate patient care in order to improve the overall quality of care and identify potential exposure to liability. By identifying and evaluating the facts and circumstances involved in all untoward events, strategies of prevention can be developed in an effort to decrease the risk of similar incidents or injuries reoccurring. Ultimately such a system should protect patients, staff, and the institution itself.

In addition to identifying actual and potential areas of liability, the incident report may identity potential litigants and assist the institution's counsel in preparing for a possible or likely lawsuit. With the knowledge of those events that might precipitate a suit, the hospital's attorney can begin planning defense strategies or proposals for a settlement offer in lieu of a trial. An incident report may also serve in apportioning blame.

Discoverability of an Incident Report

"In general, the arguments used to attempt to protect the material generated by incident reports have been peer review privilege, the attorney-client privilege, or the attorney work product privilege, which includes preparation in anticipation of litigation. The scope of these protections vary depending upon local statutes, court rules, and case law" (Fiesta 1994, 17).

In many states an incident report is considered to be confidential—a privileged communication between an institution and its legal counsel. The courts in the various states have examined the matter of the discoverability of the incident report and its admissibility as evidence in malpractice litigation. Rulings have varied, and there have been no consistent conclusions. There have been an increasing number of rulings that permit plaintiffs the right of discovery provided they can demonstrate a legitimate need. More and more courts are opening incident reports to discovery and scrutiny. Many insurance companies and agencies of federal and state government are exercising rights to secure and review them in their fiduciary and regulatory capacities.

As noted previously, an incident report should *never* be mentioned in a physician's or nurse's notes. If this were done, the legal doctrine of "incorporation by reference" can be claimed by the plaintiff's attorney. If the paralegal notes that any practitioner has stated in his or her notes that an incident report has been prepared and filed, this reference incorporates that document into the medical record and thus makes it discoverable. Any reference to the report in the record can strip away its veil of secrecy and could provide the plaintiff's lawyer with an opportunity to obtain and view what could be an asset to their case.

Any incident that causes injury or could have caused injury to *anyone*—patient, staff, visitor—on the premises of a health care facility should, without exception, require the filing of an incident report. In such instances, it is a foregone conclusion that one has been filed and exists somewhere. It is virtually never mentioned anywhere in a patient's medical record—but it is out there somewhere. In analyzing the medical record and other documents, the reviewer should look for certain "clues" as to the existence of an incident report. These may include:

- Any entries or language in the notes indicating possible liability?
- Any entries or language in the notes indicating an incident report or an untoward event. Is an incident report "advertised" in any way?
- Identification of all possible discoverable occurrences, events, situations,

- Does the P&P manual require preparation of an incident report?
- Does the manual require that incident reports be documented in the progress notes? (This is highly unlikely.)
- What is the facility's descriptive name for the incident report form?
- Are risk management reviews and reports accessible and discoverable? If accessible, is there any language indicating possible liability?

If an incident report is eventually obtained, the examiner should determine if any actual untoward events are fully, objectively, and accurately documented, including all witnesses—ancillary staff, volunteers, transport, social workers, clergy, family, visitors, and anyone else who could possibly have been involved.

REFERENCES

Cournoyer, Carmelle P. 1995. How to protect yourself legally after a patient is injured. *Nursing95 Career Directory* (January): 18–23.

Fiesta, Janine. 1994. Incident reports: Confidential or not? *Nursing Management* 25 (10): 17–18.

Sharpe, Charles C. 1999. *Nursing Malpractice: Liability and Risk Management*. Auburn House.

11

The Summary Report

PURPOSE OF THE REPORT

The primary purpose of summarizing medical records in claims of malpractice is to provide a concise, objective description of injuries allegedly suffered, and the circumstances surrounding the event, as documented in the claimant's medical records. The summary report will facilitate more immediate access to key information necessary for the preparation and prosecution of a case.

PREPARING THE REPORT

The notes that the reviewer compiles during the review and analysis of the record will form the basis of his or her summary report. If his or her notes are organized, complete, and accurate the notes may serve as an initial draft. For the paralegal, the type and format of the report that he or she will prepare will usually follow the directives and policies of the individual attorney and/or the firm. The attorney may ask for a brief oral summary, or he or she may ask for a written report, concise or lengthy. Computer software may be available to format the report. There are a number of programs for preparing "timeline" reports.

FORMAT OF THE REPORT

The timeline summary is the most common format and one of the most important and useful. This is a chronological summary, in narrative form, of the treatments, procedures, diagnostic tests, and all of the other events surrounding the incident alleged to have caused the injury. The format includes the dates, times, and all other relevant details of: (1) the events immediately preceding the incident, (2) the incident itself, and (3) the events immediately following the incident.

The preparer should include a brief description of each significant event, and include the name and page number of each document cited—this will facilitate cross-checking. In preparing a chronological narrative the report should, of course, focus on the time surrounding the incident. All information relevant to the incident must be included. Specific details may be limited in the record. The names of all parties involved, particularly any possible witnesses, should be noted. These could include the patient's visitors, the patient's roommate, and their visitors.

Include a written transcription, or a photocopy, of all relevant progress notes and other documents—particularly when there is any question of a diagnosis, meaning of terms, or legibility. Compare information from different records, documents, or other case materials. The purpose is to define similarities, differences, and identify inconsistencies and contradictions. Note any discrepancies or points that need further investigation or clarification. The paralegal should bring any inconsistencies or contradictions to the attorney's attention. Confirm all information, statements, and allegations derived from initial interviews, interrogatories, and depositions. This is why it is important to have already reviewed all case materials to correlate thoroughly and completely.

Compare the documentation in the record to the materials in discovery, that is, the statements and allegations in the case. Look for a relationship between documented data, actions, and events—particularly a causal relationship, a proximate cause. Confirm that all dates and times are consistent throughout the record. Note any significant, unexplained gaps in the progress notes or the chronology of events.

QUESTIONS THAT SHOULD BE ASKED AND ANSWERED

The report should address and answer a number of key questions. It may, in itself, raise more questions.

- Who, what, when, where, how, and why?
- Does there appear to have been an incident of malpractice?
- Was it malpractice or could it have been an accident—a "maloccurance," a "medical misadventure"?
- Was there an injury?
- Could the occurrence have caused the injury?

- Did the occurrence cause the injury?
- What was the nature and degree of the injury?
- Are there any secrets? Does it appear that anyone is trying to cover anything up?
- Are there any statements or language that impute liability?
- What is the patient's current status and prognosis?
- Could there be any other possible defendants?
- Could there be any other possible witnesses?
- Does the record indicate any basis for claim(s) other than the present one?

The final report must confirm that the reviewer has addressed each of the required elements of malpractice. The paralegal must confirm to the attorney that he or she has thoroughly reviewed all of the records relevant to the parties—the plaintiff and defendant—and all of the actual or potential issues involved.

GUIDELINES FOR PREPARATION

In preparing the final report, a number of guidelines are suggested.

- Be objective.
- Be accurate.
- Be repetitious. Reinforce important concepts, points, and terms.
- Be specific, avoid generalizations.
- Be comprehensive.
- Be concise.
- Focus on principal issues. Don't dilute the case and report by trying to address each and every point.
- Be flexible. You will not win every point.
- Try to identify those facts that may not be indicated in the records.
- Point out anything that is either beneficial or damaging to your case.
- Tell the whole story—the good side and the bad side—not what you think the attorney or client wants to hear.
- Anticipate the opposing side's arguments, positions, ploys—address them.
- Think like the opposition. Define their possible strategy.

- Identify any other providers mentioned in the file whose records might be relevant and that have not been obtained.
- Bring any inconsistencies or contradictions to the attorney's attention.
- Identify any additional possible interrogatory or deposition questions.

In using a computer to prepare reports and summaries, copy between documents to ensure consistency in language, terms, names, dates, and times. This will also save time. Many reviewers format in "landscape" style for adequate layout. This usually involves four columns:(1) date, (2) time, (3) narrative description of the events, and (4) source document—cross-referenced to the name and page number of the particular document cited.

PRESENTATION OF THE REPORT

The paralegal's report to the attorney should include:

- A cover sheet that states: "ATTORNEY WORK PRODUCT: CONFIDENTIAL";
- an outline of the contents;
- a running head: that is, "Medical Record Review of (client name)";
- a glossary—this may be optional;
- an index (optional);
- a list of all documents and records reviewed; (include page numbers, document numbers, source, and name);
- a list of relevant references and photocopies of selected references—cross-referenced to medical record page numbers;
- an itemized list of questions or points to be explored further and any additional documents to be obtained; and
- an abstract.

THE ABSTRACT

The summary report should conclude with an abstract. This should provide a quick reference, a brief synopsis of the total content of the report. It may include the reviewer's comments, opinions on factual matters, and recommendations for further action. It should include a brief recitation of all critical points and unanswered questions. It must point out anything that is either beneficial or potentially damaging to the case. Particular attention should be given to any medical complications or ongoing problems mentioned or indicated in the record. As the report itself is being prepared, the reviewer can simultaneously prepare the abstract by highlighting the most significant items to be included in it.

12

Expert Witnesses and Consultants

EXPERT WITNESSES/TESTIFYING EXPERTS

This chapter will be primarily of interest to the paralegal who may be assigned the task of locating and preparing expert witnesses for either the plaintiff or defendant. It is also intended to educate the layperson, particularly a plaintiff, about the role of such experts.

In most medical malpractice cases, the testimony of expert witnesses will be required. The role of such a witness is to educate the attorney, and the court, and to facilitate the jury's understanding of the technical, scientific, and often highly complex issues and procedures that would normally be beyond the experience or understanding of the average layperson.

The exception to the requirement for expert witnesses is the "Common Knowledge Doctrine" that provides for the exclusion of expert testimony at a trial where the facts or events of the case are such that any intelligent person would understand them. There is no need for specialized knowledge of medical or nursing procedures, technology, language, or concepts. It is assumed that the members of the jury have a sufficient degree of general knowledge and experience to comprehend the facts and issues of the case. These are such that the jury can determine that malpractice has or has not occurred without a definition by an expert. The doctrine of *res ipsa loquitur* may also be involved in such instances.

The expert witness is a professional with a calibre of training, experience, and advanced education in his or her field that distinguishes him or her from a layperson. The paralegal or lay reviewer is advised to remember that in the absence of a reasonable degree of personal medical or nursing education and professional experience, his or her own role is not to interpret the quality of medical and/or nursing care that had been provided to the patient. In their assignment of reviewing and analyzing the client's medical record, the primary task is to *summarize* the relevant information that appears in the record. It is not the function or role of the analyst to decide if malpractice has occurred—that is, to determine if there has been a breach in the standards of care. That is the role of the expert witness—the testifying expert (TE). The reviewer may draw his or her own conclusions and form his or her own personal convictions, but a final definition will be the prerogative of the expert. A final determination of malpractice will be the judgment of a court.

This does not mean that the reviewer should not be knowledgeable about basic medical and nursing procedures or fail to refer to appropriate references or resources for definitions and explanations. Such knowledge will prove invaluable in the process of review and analysis; lack of it could hinder the process. As the medical record is analyzed, the reviewer will be able to identify those entries and parts of the record that will require the assistance and expertise of an expert witness or consulting expert (CE)—physician or nurse—in analyzing and interpreting the highly scientific or technical information and data. Other experts may also be necessary to provide a comprehensive evaluation of short-and long-term effects of the injury—the medical, social, and economic implications of a prolonged period of rehabilitation and the prognosis of recovery or permanent disability.

The plaintiff usually must present expert witnesses. The defense will invariably call them also. The Federal Rules of Evidence govern the admissibility of evidence in federal courts. Under Federal Rule of Evidence 706(d) the parties may call "expert witnesses of their own selection." Other relevant Federal Rules of Evidence are shown below. State rules—which usually derive from federal rules—apply in state courts.

FEDERAL RULES OF EVIDENCE
ARTICLE VII. OPINIONS AND EXPERT TESTIMONY

Rule 701. Opinion Testimony by Lay Witnesses

If the witness is not testifying as an expert, the witness' testimony in the form of opinions or inferences is limited to those opinions or inferences which are (a) rationally based on the perception of the witness and (b) helpful to a clear understanding of the witness' testimony or the determination of a fact in issue.

Rule 702. Testimony by Experts

If scientific, technical, or other specialized knowledge will assist the trier of fact to understand the evidence or to determine a fact in issue, a witness qualified as an expert by knowledge, skill, experience, training, or education, may testify thereto in the form of an opinion or otherwise.

Rule 703. Bases of Opinion Testimony by Experts

The facts or data in the particular case upon which an expert bases an opinion or inference may be those perceived by or made known to the expert at or before the hearing. If of a type reasonably relied upon by experts in the particular field in forming opinions or inferences upon the subject, the facts or data need not be admissible in evidence.

Rule 705. Disclosure of Facts or Data Underlying Expert Opinions

The expert may testify in terms of opinion or inference and give reasons therefore without first testifying to the underlying facts or data, unless the court requires otherwise. The expert may in any event be required to disclose the underlying facts or data on cross-examination.

Selecting Expert Witnesses

The choice of expert witnesses will depend on the nature of the injury the client alleges. It will be determined by the extent and complexity of his or her medical problems and the procedures and treatments involved in the medical management of his or her illness or injury. When the need for an expert has been confirmed, it must then be determined:

- What type of expert is needed—physician, pathologist, nurse, psychiatrist?
- What medical, nursing, or other specialties or subspecialties might be required?
- What are the necessary qualifications of the expert?
- Will his or her credentials be as good as, or better than, those of opposing witnesses?
- Will he or she be considered truly "expert" or could this expert be easily impeached by the opposition?
- Where and how will the expert be located and recruited?

Locating Expert Witnesses

Expert witnesses will usually not be located in the immediate geographical area. Physicians and nurses are generally very reluctant to testify against members of their professions who practice within a defined distance from their own area, and many practitioners elect to decline their services in cases when they are asked to testify for a plaintiff. Testifying for a defendant in their own locale may be more acceptable. Typically, the expert witness will come from another city or county, if not from another state—usually at some distance away. It is not recommended that referrals be sought from physicians affiliated with local hospitals or medical practices.

Most litigation law firms maintain lists of testifying and consulting experts whom they have retained (or encountered) in previous cases and found effective. Those seeking these services are advised to avoid "hired guns." These are the individuals who actively market their services in advertisements in various legal publications or in mailings to trial attorneys. Many of them make careers out of testifying. Their reputations usually precede them. The attorney for each side will have done his or her homework in discovery. Possible sources for expert witnesses are shown in the inset below.

LOCATING EXPERT WITNESSES

- The patient/plaintiff's physician may recommend former professors, colleagues, or specialists in the field of medicine involved in the case.
- College or university faculty in medicine, nursing, or other relevant sciences can be approached.
- University affiliated teaching hospitals may be a resource.
- Networking with other trial attorneys and colleagues who might be members of bar associations or trial lawyers' associations can produce referrals. These associations may maintain registries of various kinds of expert witnesses.
- Medical and nursing professional societies or organizations may maintain lists.
- Various published medical directories that list board certified physicians, for example, *Best's Expert Witness Directory* can be consulted.
- The American Medical Association publishes various directories and maintains databases on physicians.
- Various legal publications—local bar associations and legal newspapers and journals may contain advertisements for services by reputable professionals.

- Authors of relevant textbooks or articles in professional journals may be approached.
- Contacts made at regional or national conferences in medicine, nursing, or law can be utilized.
- Agencies or individuals that advertise such services (caution about the "hired gun").
- Various federal, state, or local government departments or agencies may make experts available for testimony.
- There are a number of expert witness web sites, for example, "Expertnet" from WESTLAW, or WitnessNet, an on-line service of the Legal Research Network (LERN), which can be accessed. (See appendix I.)

Qualifications of the Expert Witness

When an attorney intends to offer the testimony of an expert in court, he or she must follow certain legal formalities in order to have such testimony accepted at the trial. It must be first established that the expert has the proper experience and expertise. The opposing counsel may ask to stipulate that the witness is qualified. This is done when the expert is clearly qualified and opposing counsel would prefer that the jury not dwell on the witness' qualifications. If the defense does not stipulate to the witness' qualifications, the expert witness must then present them and justify his or her designation as "expert."

No matter how impeccable the credentials of an expert witness, the opposing side will usually try to portray him or her as a hired gun—as a "professional" witness—and will attempt to discredit the expertise of any or all of the opposing side's witnesses. Inevitably, there will be the same conflict and disagreement between the parties in a lawsuit as to what constitutes an "expert" witness as to the credibility and merits of the expert's testimony and opinions.

An attorney may attempt to discredit the suitability of the opposition's proposed TE by disparaging his or her education, experience, expertise, or motives—any or of all of these. Each side will be challenged to show that each of their expert witnesses is a professional, expert practitioner rather than a professional, expert witness.

The individual will be questioned extensively regarding his or her prior services as a TE, the time they may devote to providing this service, and the total amount of remuneration they have received in the past and expect to receive in this case. In this instance, the TE will be challenged to assert that they are being compensated appropriately for their expertise and valuable time in testifying and not being "paid" to testify. The objective of this whole demeaning exercise is to demonstrate that the individual presented is not truly an expert, is not suitable to serve as such in the matter at issue, and therefore, should be disqualified.

The credentials of a testifying expert must be at least equal to, if not superior to, those of the individual practitioner against whom he or she is testifying. Both sides usually demand this. Their opinions will inevitably contradict one another. Their definitions and opinions are likely to be mutually exclusive. Ultimately a judge may determine if a TE is qualified to testify in court.

> The testimony of expert witnesses is inevitably theater. Jurors have no alternative but to judge the testimony of expert witnesses on the personal credibility of the witness. Positive factors such as academic degrees, specialty board certification, and publications influence credibility. So do factors such as physical appearance, race, gender, command of English, and personality. For an expert witness, the foremost qualifications are effective presentation and teaching ability. The expert must educate the jury. . . . The objective is to convince the jurors that they understand the technical issues. Once there is a perception of understanding, the expert can convince them that they are making an independent decision that his or her testimony is correct rather than just agreeing with him or her. (Richards and Rathbun 1993, 141)

> Sometimes after the smoke clears and the dueling experts have put away their guns away, the most injured body left on the courtroom floor is the one called science. . . . Maybe the experts were mercenaries with opinions for hire. . . . More and more frequently, a legal verdict about right or wrong hinges on a scientific judgment of true or false. Yet, judges and juries, the scientific laity that we count on for justice, often come to complex cases as poorly prepared as a sixth-grader faced with quantum physics. . . . As science and the law come into contact and conflict, the courts need their own neutral experts. They need the scientific community to help separate the science from the fiction . . . these moves come from the recognition that bad science makes bad law. . . . [The] courts are replete with "experts" who give "what is charitably called an educated guess." Meanwhile the adversarial nature of the courtroom alienates many of the best scientists. They don't want to testify in a courtroom they regard as more like a theater than a lab. (Goodman 1998, A11)

An attorney, in a misguided effort to promote the best case for their client, may assume that any TE should know all there is about medicine or nursing, and he or she might attempt to exert some pressure or offer an attractive incentive to a prospective witness. The individual approached in this situation would be obliged to refuse any case involving issues beyond his or her area of expertise. Should they comply, they could be doing a great disservice to themselves, to their profession, and certainly to a plaintiff or defendant. However, he or she might still serve the attorney and his or her own profession effectively by assisting in locating a more qualified expert to serve a client's best interest.

The TE can not have any direct relationship or connection with any of the parties in the case. There can be no hint of conflict of interest; otherwise, the TE's credibility could be impeached. In accepting a case, the expert witness must be willing to determine, and judge, the merits of the case, and withdraw or commit according to his or her convictions. Agreeing to testify, assuming that role, is tantamount to full endorsement of the case and the client's position. Should convictions and commitment change for any reason, the TE may exercise his or her right to withdraw services.

Role of the Expert Witness

In cases of professional negligence (unintentional torts) standards of care are most relevant. They are not relevant in intentional torts. Expert witnesses are usually required in malpractice claims to interpret the appropriate standards of medical or nursing care. The expert witness *does not establish* the standards of care but rather *elucidates* them—for the attorneys, the jury, and the court. His or her function is to educate, to propound to the court the standards of care that would have been expected and required in the circumstances of the alleged incident of malpractice, and to provide an *opinion* that the defendant met or did not meet those standards. *The opinions and inferences of expert witnesses are admissible as evidence.*

Standards of medical care must be addressed by physicians and those of nursing, by nurses. The defense attorney for a practitioner accused of malpractice would likely protest a physician testifying as to the standards of nursing care (or conversely) unless the procedure under consideration involves a skill or function that either a physician or a nurse may routinely perform. This situation has become more common in the climate of nursing practice today.

The opinions offered by the expert will be based on the information revealed to the expert in discovery and in review and analysis of the client's medical record. Much of the testimony of the expert will be directly relevant to the content of the medical record or will consist of answers to hypothetical questions. The TE is not a "witness to the facts." He or she does not testify about or address the veracity or actual occurrence of the factual matters of the case. He or she will be asked to provide opinions and interpretations of the alleged facts or other information as presented; whereas a witness to the facts will testify from the perspective of one who actually saw the alleged incident or participated in the event directly or indirectly.

The Expert Witness' Report

The expert witness' report is a memo summarizing his or her opinions and findings. The value of these will depend on the preparation of the TE. It is essential to prepare specific interview questions that will address the issues of the case. This will anticipate his or her expected performance at a deposition and trial. In the preparation of a TE, the paralegal should direct responses and opinions to the medical probability, not the possibility.

Federal Rule of Civil Procedure 26(a)(2)(B) relates to the production of expert reports. Under this rule, these must be produced for all experts who have been retained to provide expert testimony at the trial or have been employed by a party and whose regular duties involve the provision of such testimony.

All such reports must be prepared by the expert themselves and not by the attorney who has retained them. The report must be in writing and signed by the expert. This effectively circumvents the practice in which attorneys directed their testifying experts to present their findings in an oral report in order to prevent discovery by opposing counsel. The *consulting* expert is, as we shall discuss in a following section, exempt from this rule since his or her reports are considered attorney work product and nondiscoverable.

Under Federal Rule of Civil Procedure 26(a)(2) each party must disclose to the other the names of any expert witnesses who may be called to testify during the trial. These disclosures must ordinarily be made at least ninety days prior to the date of the trial. The following information about each expert witness must be disclosed in a statement that is signed by the witness:

- A statement by each witness of the opinions he or she will express, the bases for these, and the information or data used to frame their opinions;
- any exhibits that will be utilized to define, clarify, or support opinions;
- the professional qualifications of each expert witness;
- a listing of all publications authored by the expert within the past ten years;

- the amount of compensation that each will receive; and
- a listing of all cases in which each has testified as an expert at a deposition or trial, within a prior four-year period.

THE CONSULTING EXPERT

The role of the consulting expert is somewhat different from that of the testifying expert, and the research, findings, and reports of the CE enjoy a degree of privilege not afforded to the TE.

Role of the Consulting Expert

Unlike the TE, the consulting expert does not testify at deposition or trial. He or she only consults, as their title indicates. This service may be provided for either side in a lawsuit. The TE may initially assist as consulting expert; however, his or her role and focus is considerably narrower than that of the CE. The testimony of the TE will be confined to the area of his or her expertise or clinical specialty. He or she may be permitted only limited access to the medical record or other discovery documents. The CE can take a much broader approach to a case and usually has unlimited access to the medical record and all other pertinent materials. In this capacity, the CE can review and assess the actions of any and all health care providers who were involved in the patient's care and address any one of a large number of cogent and peripheral issues. They adopt a global rather than a regional approach to a case—generalist rather than specialist.

In their role they can provide a variety of litigation support services to an attorney in the malpractice trial preparation process and during a trial. As a consulting expert to either plaintiff or defense attorney, he or she acts as a collaborator and strategist. Since less than 10 percent of all malpractice lawsuits ever go to trial, the CE's value is in helping to prepare a sound case, the merits of which could induce an offer of prompt and reasonable settlement by the opposition and thus reduce the costs of a prolonged suit. There are a number of advantages in the utilization of CEs: (1) They are experts in their professional practice, (2) they know the standards of care for their profession, and (3) they have the superior advantage of hindsight.

Some of the ongoing support services that the consulting or testifying expert can provide in collaboration with the attorney and/or the paralegal in prescreening cases, pretrial preparations, and trial support are shown below.

SERVICES THAT THE CONSULTING EXPERT MAY PROVIDE

Overall Collaboration

- Collaborate with the attorney, paralegals, other staff, and the client in case preparation and strategy for the best possible case.
- Act as liaison between parties, physicians, and attorneys.
- Enhance communication between all parties in efforts for successful resolution of case.
- Provide ongoing support and availability in the litigation process from pretrial preparation through trial.

Initial Review and Screening of Cases

- Evaluate records and advise attorney on merits of a case.
- Identify cases with merit or those with no merit. Weed out weak cases.
- Assist in a decision to pursue a case.
- Evaluate potential for effective defense or prosecution.
- Spot potential trouble cases early.
- Assist in initial assessment of issues of damages, causation, and potential liability.
- Assist in assessing damages/injuries.
- Mitigate damages, claims, suits, and awards in determining potential liability.
- Help in development of theories of liability.
- Forewarn attorney to avoid arguing indefensible points.
- Help eliminate surprises.

Witnesses—Identifying, Locating, Interviewing, Preparing

- Assist in identifying and locating potential witnesses and defendants.
- Participate with attorney and paralegal in interviewing clients and witnesses.
- Assist in the preparation of witnesses for deposition and trial testimony.
- Aid in preparing questions and responses in depositions and trial.
- Define the qualifications of TE and CE.
- Identify and evaluate expert witnesses.

- Utilize an extensive, nationwide network of resources.
- Assume time consuming searches.
- Locate, communicate, and confer with the most qualified experts.
- Assist in negotiations for their services.
- Network with professional, expert colleagues in practice or academia.

Discovery

- Assist in the preparation of interrogatories, complaints, and other appropriate documents and responses to them.
- Suggest other possible areas of investigation.
- Assist in preparation of client or witnesses for deposition.
- Assist in preparation of deposition questions.
- Review and summarize deposition transcripts.

Education

- Inform attorneys and other parties on facts and issues relevant to medical or nursing care.
- Validate the knowledge and understanding of all parties.
- Provide a comprehensive perspective on all issues.
- Identify all possible critical incidents and facts.
- Define the relevant professional standards of care.
- Identify any deviations from the standards of care.
- Define the nature and extent of alleged injuries.
- Explore, identify, and define the possible ramifications of the injuries.
- Utilize professional knowledge base as resource.
- Define and simplify medical and nursing terminology and procedures.
- Conduct seminars for attorney's staff on appropriate topics and issues.
- Advise on all health care related issues and multitude of relevant topics.

Medical Records Review

- Organize, review, and analyze the medical records.
- Prepare summaries, chronologies, reports of all pertinent facts, incidents, and issues according to the attorney's preference.
- Provide an initial assessment of the plaintiff's alleged injuries.
- Review relevant reports generated by opposition's experts.
- Correlate findings with client's TE reports.
- Identify specific areas that do not support attorney-client's case.
- Compare and correlate all findings to the allegations and issues.
- Alert attorney to deficient records or suspected tampering.
- Prepare glossaries, indexes, and other references.
- Identify missing records.
- Assist in obtaining all pertinent records and documents.

Research

- Provide depth and enhance the scope and breadth of information relevant to the case.
- Conduct medical library and on-line database searches.
- Identify, locate, and retrieve the most current, authoritative, and pertinent literature available.
- Review, analyze, summarize, and integrate all relevant literature.
- Conduct conferences to present, review, and clarify research findings.
- Provide attorney-client with compilations of relevant materials.
- Assist in the construction of databases and in computer scanning and storage of documents.
- Assist the attorney-client in setting up or improving the medical reference materials in the firm's library.
- Recommend appropriate publications—textbooks, journals, periodicals, and standard reference works.
- Conduct field trips to the site of the incident.
- Prepare or locate and obtain exhibits or other demonstrative evidence including videotapes, computer software, CDs, models, equipment, and charts.

Cost Saving

- Utilization of consultants can expedite and simplify the process of case preparation and trial.
- Cost effective for an attorney to use CE to screen, analyze, and prepare a well-researched and well-conducted case.
- Prepares and provides focused, detailed information and direction to maximize effectiveness, productivity, and efficiency.
- CE's knowledge base reduces time attorney and/or staff might otherwise require in preparation and research.
- Attorney can turn tedious, routine tasks over to CE. This allows the attorney and his or her staff to focus on the important legal aspects of case.
- Save the attorney-client and firm time and money and maximize his or her return, value, profits, and bottom line.

Discoverability of the Consulting Expert's Work

The testifying expert has a high and visible profile while presenting testimony during a deposition or a trial. The consulting expert is "invisible," working covertly behind the scenes in a clandestine collaboration with the attorney from the initial phases of the case right on through any eventual trial. Any report generated by the CE is considered "attorney's work product," and as such is usually privileged and confidential. Unless a testifying expert incorporates any or all of a report generated by a CE into his or her own discoverable testimony, a CE's report is generally not discoverable. His or her thoughts and opinions are protected from scrutiny by the cloak of anonymity that the role imparts.

Generally, the consultant's work product and his or her identity are not discoverable until, and if, the consultant agrees to serve as an expert witness. Any reports generated prior to that transition would not necessarily become discoverable. In these instances, the paralegal is advised to check all appropriate sources for rules of procedure, applicable statutes, and relevant case law. In working with a CE or a TE, the paralegal is advised to keep all written correspondence to a minimum. Either expert should be directed to submit written reports to the attorney only when such are specifically requested. And the consultant expert should be advised not to make any notations in any document that would be considered discoverable.

"Parties are not required to identify experts acting solely as consulting or non-testifying experts. Their identities, reports, and facts known or opinions held are discoverable only under exceptional circumstances.

These circumstances are generally identified as situations under which it is impracticable for the party seeking discovery to obtain the facts of opinions on the same subject by any other means" Federal Rules of Civil Procedure 26(b)(4)(B).

The Qualifications of the Consulting Expert

Like the expert witness, the litigation consultant's credentials, ethical standards, and integrity must be above reproach. However, the CE may work on any type of case and perform a variety of services, regardless of the medical or nursing specialty involved. The issues may involve injury, illness, or health. In reviewing the medical records, the CE can draw on his or her own knowledge, skills, experience, and education in identifying and reporting the issues involved. However, an expert in any given specialty should be consulted as the need arises. It would be reckless and presumptuous for any CE to present him-or herself as an expert in all areas of medical or nursing practice. No one can know, or credibly pretend to know, everything about his or her profession and all of its specialties and subspecialties.

PROFESSIONAL NURSES AS CONSULTING EXPERTS

Many trial attorneys have increased the utilization of registered nurses as CEs (and as TEs where nursing malpractice is at issue). For a discussion of professional nurses in these roles the reader is referred to Sharpe 1999, chapter 16.

Using nurses rather than physicians represents a very cost effective way for a lawyer to prepare a personal injury or malpractice case. As a specialist, the nurse consultant is unique to both the nursing and the legal professions and plays an integral role in each.

The nurse as litigation consultant is usually a licensed registered nurse who performs a critical analysis of health care delivery and its outcomes as a service to the legal profession. With appropriate and extensive education—preferably a master's degree or higher—and clinical experience, the nurse, as consultant, is an expert in the standards of nursing practice and thus qualified to assess any deviations in such standards as might have occurred in clinical nursing practice or other health care situations.

In this role, a nurse may practice in a variety of settings, including law firms, government agencies, insurance companies, hospitals and other health care institutions, and in independent professional practice. In this capacity, the nurse acts as a liaison between the legal and health care professions. He or she functions as a resource to the attorney and the attorney's professional staff. It is a function of the nurse litigation consultant to provide consultation and education to legal professionals in such issues as medical malpractice, nursing malpractice, personal injury, disability claims, product liability, workers' compensation, toxic torts, and matters of professional nursing licensure. The primary role of the nurse litigation consultant is to evaluate, analyze, and render informed expert opinions on the delivery of health care and the outcomes of such care. The suggested qualifications of the nurse as TE or CE are shown below.

THE QUALIFICATIONS OF A NURSE AS AN EXPERT WITNESS OR CONSULTING EXPERT

- The nurse is, in fact, an expert in his or her field—indisputably.
- He or she holds a current license to practice in one or more states. (The nurse does not have to be licensed in the state in which he or she will consult or testify.)
- The TE or CE nurse's professional credentials should match or exceed those of any defendant nurse's.
- The TE or CE should have the appropriate nursing education. An attorney may require a BSN as a minimum level of academic preparation. Many demand a master's degree.
- The nurse has acquired sufficient, relevant, and *current* clinical experience. This should be a minimum of five years in the specialty area that the TE or CE is addressing in the case.
- He or she hold certification in a specialty area of nursing. A clinical nurse specialist (CNS), nurse practitioner (NP), or other advanced practice nurse (APN) is the most suitable expert witness.
- The TE or CE should hold other professional credentials including faculty in nursing education, publication, speaking, honors and awards, and membership in appropriate professional organizations.
- The candidate has a reasonably thorough understanding of the legal system and the legal issues in malpractice. Many TEs and CEs are also paralegals. Many are nurse attorneys.
- The TE or CE should be thoroughly familiar with the nurse practice act, and all related rules and regulations, in the state that will have jurisdiction in the case for which he or she is called to testify.

REFERENCES

Goodman, Ellen. 1998. Courts need neutral experts to separate fact from fiction. *The Morning Call* (February 24): A11.

Richards, Edward P., and Katharine Rathbun. 1993. *Law and the Physician: A Practical Guide.* Little Brown and Co. (An electronic book, online.)

Sharpe, Charles C. 1999. *Nursing Malpractice: Liability and Risk Management.* Auburn House.

13

Cybercare and Medical Records

TELEHEALTH: TELEMEDICINE, TELENURSING

There has been increasing discussion in both the general and professional media about telecommunications technology and its applications to the rapidly developing concept of "telemedicine." The terms telemedicine and "telehealth" are often blurred and used interchangeably. The former, which has been used most frequently, actually refers to a subset of the more inclusive telehealth, which is becoming the preferred terminology because it more accurately represents the current model of health care delivery with its focus on health maintenance, wellness, and disease prevention. Telehealth embraces clinical care of various kinds—including "telenursing." Additionally, the concept encompasses the related areas of the education of health professionals and the health care consumer, public health, research, and the administration and management of the provision of a variety of other health services. For purposes of our discussion here, "telemedicine" and "telehealth" will be used interchangeably.

Telehealth Defined

"Telehealth is the linking of two or more end-user sites by any interactive electronic means for the purpose of transmission and/or exchange of information and data in any health-related application. It is remote, electronic, clinical consultation, assessment, and monitoring of consumers of any form of health care. Telehealth is the utilization of telecommunications technology in the dissemination of health information, expertise, and intervention across varying distances to a disparate population most often in greatest need of such access" (Sharpe 1999, chapter 15).

Telemedicine provides a variety of services to the patient, including:

- Access to remote health care practitioners in real time;
- retrieval and transmission of medical records and data;
- consultation, assessment, and diagnosis of physical or mental illness or conditions;
- implementation and management of a medical regimen of treatment; and
- ongoing remote monitoring of the effectiveness of that regimen and the patient's response and status.

The United States Departments of Commerce and Health and Human Services Joint Working Group on Telemedicine (JWGT) in the *Telemedicine Report to Congress* January 31, 1997, stated in the opening message from Secretary Cantor:

> Telemedicine has the potential to make a difference in the lives of many Americans. In rural areas where a patient and the closest health professional can be hundreds of miles apart, telemedicine can provide access to health care where little had been available before. In emergency cases, this access can mean the difference between life and death. In particular, in those cases where fast medical response time and specialty care are needed, telemedicine availability could be critical.
>
> In addition, telemedicine can improve the delivery of health care to Americans by bringing a wider range of services . . . to the underserved. It can also help attract and retain health professionals in rural areas by providing ongoing training and collaboration with other health professionals.
>
> Key issues that must be settled before telemedicine can proliferate include: the licensure of telemedicine health professionals who work across state lines or who provide services on a multi-state basis; telemedicine safety and standards issues relating to the relative lack of standards in this field; the lack of insurer payment for telemedicine services; privacy and security issues unique to telemedicine; and the telecommunications infrastructure cost and accessibility for telemedicine use.

Telemedicine, in one form or another, has actually been practiced for over thirty years. At the most simple level, a nurse providing clinical advice or triage over the telephone is telemedicine. The focus of the most recent activity, however, has been on telemedicine applications that generally employ advanced image and audio capabilities. These technologies can range from high resolution still images (e.g., X-rays) to sophisticated interactive teleconferencing systems.

Issues and Questions

The problem that telehealth presents is that the revolution in science and technology has run ahead of the devolution of law. The legal system has not yet caught up. The courts and the regulatory bodies have not kept pace. A key issue that has just begun to be addressed by state boards of medicine and nursing is the legality of providing health care across state lines—an inherent aspect of telehealth. Are nurses and physicians who are participating in "modem medicine" violating the laws of the states in which they are licensed to practice by, in effect, practicing across state lines? Are they violating the laws of those states in which their remote patients reside—and in which they are not licensed (Gobis 1996; Kjervik 1997)?

There have been proposals—all rejected out-of-hand—that in a scenario of telemedicine, the patient has simply "relocated," traveled electronically through cyberspace to the location of the provider. The clinical site is now there and the legal jurisdiction is effectively established there. But could the converse not also be true? The practitioner is teleported to the patient. These arguments are considered specious at best.

Telecommunications has created, and certainly will continue to create, new questions, problems, and challenges to the medical and nursing professions and their regulators. The most germane questions are: Is telemedicine medical practice? The consensus is that if such health care services are delivered by any means, it constitutes the practice of medicine. Is telenursing nursing practice? Yes! This has been affirmed by the National Council of State Boards of Nursing (1997, 1).

The legal issues can be grouped under three broad categories: (1) those that are not unique to telemedicine, for example, tort and criminal law, malpractice; (2) conflicts in state laws that arise in the provision of interstate services, for example, the issue of licensure; and (3) those inherent in the concept of telemedicine itself, for example, privacy in cyberspace.

- In the event of a malpractice lawsuit, where will ultimate legal jurisdiction reside?

- Where will a lawsuit be filed? In the state of the patient's residence? In the several different states of licensure of any number of different practitioners?
- How will all possible defendants be identified by plaintiffs' attorneys?
- How and where will they be located and subpoenaed?
- Where and how will the plaintiff's complete medical record be located and obtained?
- When are providers of health care subject to the licensing requirements of another state? Must a practitioner be licensed in the state in which his or her intervention and/or consultation initiates and in each and every state in which it may ultimately be received? This question of interstate licensure remains unresolved by both medical and nursing regulatory authorities. It represents a significant factor in the maximum implementation and utilization of telemedicine.
- Are practitioners providing telehealth care subject to the statutes, rules, and regulations of other states, such as those regarding the reporting of communicable diseases?
- To what degree, if any, will he or she be subject to the investigative and disciplinary authority of another state's board of medicine or nursing?
- What standards of privacy will apply to the transmission of patient information? Intrastate and interstate electronic transmission of personal information creates an array of new issues and problems. Currently, federal and state regulatory agencies are challenged to determine appropriate authority and jurisdiction.
- What standards of care will be invoked and required? Will a diagnosis and treatment made via telecommunication be held to the same standards of care as one made by a practitioner in the physical presence of the patient?
- Because of the diversity of state laws, will the definition and implementation of national standards be required for interstate telemedicine?
- When is the physician-patient relationship created? When is duty established? When the practitioner comes on-line?
- What will be the roles of advanced practice nurses or physicians' assistants? Will they be legally authorized in every state to participate in telemedicine? Dependently? Independently? The state laws vary considerably.
- How will nurses and physicians determine their liability and

rights in other states, other countries? The implications for international telehealth are staggering.

- Will they be protected in all jurisdictions that their telemedical interventions reach?
- How will practitioners protect their practices and their assets from claims for damages that could arise in any state from individuals they have never personally encountered?
- How will malpractice insurance companies deal with interstate coverage if the insured is defined as a resident of a particular state? Will coverage be restricted to that state only? Is malpractice insurance portable through cyberspace?
- How will a patient keep track of and identify all of the absent and remote practitioners who may have participated in his or her care by telemedicine—their names, the dates, times, treatment regimens, orders, and many other details of their care?
- What records will be maintained by the patient or his or her immediate caregivers?
- How will informed consent be obtained when the statutory requirements for it vary among the states?
- What are the implications for advance directives? Will a remote physician be charged with implementing them without the opportunity of personal contact with the patient?
- What could happen if the system is compromised or fails at a critical moment? What are the legal implications of such an event?
- Who will be liable in the event of the electronic misappropriation of a person's medical record?
- Will a very ill or debilitated patient, or his or her caregivers, be able to effectively participate in telemedicine? How will this be determined?
- Will the average patient have the basic understanding of computer technology to participate effectively and therapeutically in telemedicine? Or will "technophobia" prevent this?

General Privacy, Confidentiality, and Security Issues in Telemedicine

Privacy advocates and telecommunications experts continue to grapple with the many issues that continue to emerge as new technology is constantly being implemented in the delivery of health care. In dealing with these issues, understanding what these terms mean is important. Privacy is the ability of an individual to control the use and dissemination of information that relates to himself or herself. Confidentiality is the primary means of protecting that privacy. Sensitive information is accorded a confidential status that mandates specific controls, including strict limitations on access and disclosure.

These controls must be adhered to by all those handling the information. Security embraces all the safeguards in a computer-based information system. Security protects both the system and the information contained within it from unauthorized access and misuse and accidental damage. Security also includes training and policies—not just technologies (e.g., "fire walls" and encryption).

Legal protection for health information generally resides at the state level. While every state has adopted some form of privacy statutes, rules, and regulations, the degree and effectiveness of protection can vary from state to state. About a dozen states have comprehensive health care information confidentiality statutes. Many state statutes govern specific classes of health information derived and maintained by public health agencies, including that relating to HIV/AIDS, mental health, and communicable diseases.

Federal protection of privacy is even more limited than that provided by the states. No explicit right to privacy is guaranteed under the Constitution; privacy protection is derived from case law. The only federal health record confidentiality law covering the nation is one controlling disclosure of an individual's substance abuse history, and only specialized substance abuse facilities and units are subject to the law. While there are a number of federal initiatives underway that examine the protection of electronic patient information, there has been little consideration given to privacy issues related specifically to telemedicine (*Telemedicine Report to Congress*, Section B).

Emerging Privacy, Confidentiality, and Security Issues in Telemedicine

Because of the unique combination of patient data, video imaging, and electronic clinical information that is generated between two distant sites during a telemedicine encounter, privacy concerns that normally pertain to patient medical records may be magnified within the telemedicine arena or may be altogether different in character, complexity, and legal implications.

Telemedicine technology is so innovative that many new privacy and security issues are just now coming to light. They include:

- A lack of uniform confidentiality and privacy legislation at the state level in terms of the transfer of health information in telemedicine encounters (just as there is with respect to health information generally).

- Since telemedicine consultations can take place over state lines, the potential for confusion over which state's standards should be employed could arise.
- A long-distance telemedicine consultation typically involves a clinician-patient session that can be videotaped in its entirety. Thus, the health professional may face his/her own privacy issues under these circumstances. For example, unlike standard medical record documentation in which the practitioner has discretion to selectively record his or her findings, most interactive telemedicine consultations are recorded in toto. This audio/video record is maintained as part of the documentation of the consultation. As a result, practitioners have less discretion to remove "sensitive" items that they might otherwise not wish in the record.
- The use of telemedicine equipment usually adds additional personnel to the typical provider-patient encounter. For instance, a technical outsider, like an engineer or webmaster, may be privy to the consultation.
- From the patient's perspective, the patient may not be able to "see" who else is viewing the session along with the clinician on the other side of the long distance consultation.
- From a technical standpoint, there is a higher volume of data and complexity involved in the various communication mediums used during a typical telemedicine consultation. That could make securing the data more problematic. (*Telemedicine Report to Congress*, Section C)

THE ELECTRONIC MEDICAL RECORD

Unlike standard medical record documentation in which the practitioner has discretion to selectively record his or her findings, most interactive telemedicine consultations are recorded in their entirety. This record usually is maintained as part of the documentation of the consultation. This is of particular concern in the use of telemedicine technologies for treating mental illness, substance abuse, and other conditions that carry a social stigma. Although issues of privacy and security in telemedicine have much in common with those regarding medical records, the use of live, interactive video introduces certain technical dimensions that must be very carefully evaluated. For example, maintenance of secure transmission lines is critical (*Telemedicine Report to Congress* 1997, Section D).

By definition, telemedicine requires the electronic transmission of a patient's medical record and its dispersion among any number of health care providers. Questions immediately present such as:

- In the event of a lawsuit for malpractice, will there be a "paper trail" or will there be only a nebulous accumulation of electronic records stored in many unknown databases, in many unknown places?
- In what format will records be maintained—paper documents, computer disks, or any other form of electronic media?
- What will constitute an "original" complete record?
- In the event of a lawsuit, where will *the* definitive copy be located?
- How many computer files and databases will have to be located and examined to confirm that the complete record has been identified?
- Will the attorney, paralegal, or lay reviewer have the advanced skills in computer technology to be able to search for, locate, and retrieve the information they need?
- Will they be able to track it down in the vastness of cyberspace?
- Who will be the ultimate custodian of the complete record—*one* file, in *one* place? Will there be *a* medical record?
- Will there be a number of custodians of discrete portions of a dispersed record in many different formats and media?
- How will those seeking the record know who is/are the custodian(s)?
- How will an individual component of the record be obtained—which state's laws will control access by the plaintiff or their attorney?
- Will the patient him-or herself have electronic access to all or any part of it on an ongoing basis? Which state's statutes will apply?
- Will he or she be able to make copies or will it be "read only"?
- How will he or she be able to verify the completeness and accuracy of the documents they might access?
- What procedures will be in place for the patient to amend, correct, or clarify a record?
- Will every participating practitioner have a complete and identical copy?
- How can the integrity of records disseminated among many providers be maintained?

- How will the credibility and integrity of any record or any document in it be proven?
- Will an electronic medical record be admissible as evidence in every court of law?
- Will there be guarantees of confidentiality and privacy? Unauthorized access and disclosure could be cause for a claim by both the patient and practitioner whose clinical skills and their documentation could be made subject to scrutiny.
- What consistent safeguards, if any, will protect the information from tampering or destruction? Data on a computer disk can be altered or destroyed with a few quick keystrokes.
- What will be the required credentials of expert witnesses who will review electronic medical records? Will they have to be computer experts? Will they be required to verify the authenticity of the data itself?

MALPRACTICE LIABILITY IN TELEMEDICINE

Medical malpractice has been previously defined as professional misconduct in improperly discharging professional duties or failing to meet the standard of care of a professional. Various definitions of "standard of care" and "professional duties" have been provided by statutes, regulations, and case law. The diverse nature of these definitions and their sources are further complicated by jurisdictional issues when applied in the area of telemedicine. The additional problem of the time delay between the event leading to a malpractice claim and the filing of the claim means that some problems may take up to two or more years before they become apparent.

Legal parameters for medical malpractice will be the same regardless of the medium or setting of patient care. If telemedicine results in negligence and injury, there will be lawsuits. It is generally agreed that telemedical consultation and treatment establishes duty and, therefore, liability on the part of every practitioner who directly participates.

At the time of this writing, the body of case law on telemedicine and its implications for malpractice was relatively scarce. There appears to be no clear guidelines regarding the implications of telemedicine and malpractice. There are many issues to be resolved and many questions to be answered. The required elements of malpractice must still be present in remote care as they are in bedside care. The practice of medicine and the practice of nursing are bound by the same professional standards no matter the medium of delivery.

Telemedicine can either increase or decrease the risk of malpractice liability—depending on one's perception. Many advocates contend that two or more practitioners collaborating can reduce the liability risks. Access to a large number of highly sophisticated medical databases will enhance diagnostic abilities and effectiveness of treatment and improve patient outcomes. The telemedicine approach to health care is more comprehensive in its ability to access experts from many disciplines on demand—immediately—from anywhere in the country or anywhere in the world.

Many also contend that improved technology could lead to improved patient expectations. And when practitioners fail to meet them, this could engender more demands and increased litigation in perceived incidents of malpractice. Practitioners will be challenged to upgrade and maintain their clinical skills to match the technology.

An excellent source for further information on telemedicine and the law can be found on the World Wide Web at: http://www.arentfox.com/telemedicine.html.

REFERENCES

Gobis, Linda J. 1996. Telenursing: Nursing by telephone across state lines. *Journal of Nursing Law* 3 (3) (March): 7–17.

Kjervik, D. K. 1997. Telenursing—licensure and communication challenges. *Journal of Professional Nursing* 13 (2) (March–April): 65.

National Council of State Boards of Nursing. 1997. *Position Paper on Telenursing: A Challenge to Regulation*: 1–2.

Sharpe, Charles C. 1999. *Nursing Malpractice: Liability and Risk Management*. Auburn House.

United States Departments of Commerce and Health and Human Services. 1997. *Telemedicine Report to Congress*. January 31. The complete text of the report is available from: http://www.ntia.doc.gov/reports/telemed/index.htm.

Appendix I

Web Sites

American Board of Medical Specialties
http://www.abms.org/

American Health Information Management Association
http://www.ahima.org/

American Health Lawyers Association
http://www.healthlawyers.org

American Institute of Medical Law
http://www.aimlaw.com/

American Medical Association (AMA)
http://www.ama-assn.org/sitemap.html

American Nurses Association
http://www.nursingworld.org/

Anatomy: Cliniweb
http://www.ohsu.edu/cliniweb/anatomy.html

Atlas of the Body: AMA
http://www.ama-assn.org/insight/gen_hlth/atlas/atlas.htm

Blood Test Guide: AMA
http://www.ama-assn.org/insight/gen_hlth/blood/blood.htm

Center for Telemedicine Law
http://www.ctl.org/

Clinical Calculator: drugs
http://www.intmed.mcw.edu/clincalc.html

Clinical Pharmacology Online
http://www.cponline.gsm.com/

CliniWeb
http://www.ohsu.edu/cliniweb/search.html

Digital Anatomist
http://www1.biostar.washington.edu/DigitalAnatomist.html

Digital Medical Library™
http://www.telemedical.com/Telemedical/library.html

Drug Formulary
http://www.intmed.mcw.edu/drug.html

FindLaw: Health Law
http://www.findlaw.com/

Galaxy
http://www.einet.net/
http://www.einet.net/galaxy/Medicine.html

Hardin Meta Directory of Internet Health Sources
http://www.arcade.uiowa.edu/hardin-www/md.html

Hardin MetaDirectory: pharmacology
http://www.lib.uiowa.edu/hardin/md/pharm.html

HealthAtoZ
http://www.healthatoz.com/

HealthExplorer
http://www.healthexplorer.com/

Health Finder: U. S. Department of Health and Human Services
htttp://www.healthfinder.gov/

Healthtouch
http://www.healthtouch.com/

Healthtouch: drug information
http://www.healthtouch.com/level1/p_dri.htm

HealthWeb
http://healthweb.org/subjABC.html

Internet Medical Resources
http://www.pslgroup.com/MEDRES.htm

Internet Resources in Health Law
http://lawlib.slu.edu/centers/hlthlaw/hlthlink.htm

Internet Sleuth: medicine, pharmacology
http://www.isleuth.com/

Laboratory Test Interpretation
http://www.neosoft.com/~uthman/lab_test.htm

Laboratory Values
http://www.ghsl.nwu.edu/Norm.html

'Lectric Law Library's Medicine and Law
http://www.lectlaw.com/tmed.html

Martindale: Medical Law
http://www-sci.lib.uci.edu/HSG/Legal.html

Mayo Clinic: diseases, conditions, tests, procedures, glossary, dictionary, drug information
http://www.mayohealth.org/mayo/common/htm/index.htm

Mayo Clinic: Internet Information Resource
http://www.mayo.edu/outlinks.html

MedExlorer
http://www.medexplorer.com/

Medical and Public Health Law Site
The Public Health Law Project
University of Missouri at Kansas City
http://www.plague.law.umkc.edu/

Medical Glossary: AMA
http://www.ama-assn.org/insight/gen_hlth/glossary/index.htm

Medical Malpractice Resource Page
http://www.helpquick.com/medmal.htm

Medical Matrix
http://www.medmatrix.org/

Medical Reference Sites
http//www.pslgroup.com/dg/medrefsites.htm

Medical World Search
http://pride-sun.poly.edu:80/MMcrawler-new2/about.html

MedicineNet: diseases, treatments, drug information, glossary, dictionary
http://www.medicinenet.com

MedMark Medical Bookmarks
http://www.medmark.org/

MedWeb: Emory University Health Sciences Center
http://www.cc.emory.edu/WHSCL/medweb.html

The Merck Manual
http://www.merck.com/

Merriam Webster Online Medical Dictionary
AOL Keyword: Merriam Webster

Multi Media Medical Reference Library: (J. Tward)
http://www.med-library.com/medlibrary

My Virtual Reference Desk
http://www.refdesk.com/health.html

National Council of State Boards of Nursing, Inc.
http://www.ncsbn.org/

National Library of Medicine
http://www.nlm.nih.gov/

National Library of Medicine: MEDLINE search
http://www.ncbi.nlm.nih.gov/PubMed

National Practitioner Data Bank
http://www.npdb.com/

Pharmacy Information on the Internet
http://www.pharminfo.net/

PharmInfoNet: Pharmaceutical Informaton Network
http://pharminfo.com/pharmlink.html
http://pharminfo.com/drugdb/db_mnu.html

Pharmlink
http://www.pharmlink.com/

Richards, Edward P., and Katharine Rathbun
Law and the Physician: A Practical Guide
http://www.plague.law.umkc.edu/xfiles/xfc.htm

Richards, Edward P., and Katharine Rathbun
Medical Risk Mangement: Preventive Legal Strategies for Health Care Providers
http://www.plague.law.umkc.edu/aspen/Aspen-Contents.html

RxList
http://www.rxlist.com.

Slack Inc.: guide to internet clinical medical resources
http://slackinc.com/
http://slackinc.com/matrix

Telemedicine Information Exchange (TIE)
http://www.tie.org/

United States Departments of Commerce and Health and Human Services *Telemedicine Report to Congress*. January 31, 1997
http://www.ntia.doc.gov/reports/telemed/index.htm

"Virtual" Medical Center
http://www.scilib.uci.edu/HSG/Medical.html

Web's Legal Dictionary (The)
http://www.wwlia.org/diction.htm

Yahoo
http://www.yahoo.com/Health/Medicine/
http://www.yahoo.com/Health/Nursing/
http://www.yahoo.com/Health/Pharmacy/Drugs

Yale New Haven Hospital: Issues in Risk Management
http://info.med.yale.edu/caim/risk/contents.html

Appendix II

State Laws on Patient Access to Medical Records

State	Physician	Hospital	Mental Health Records
Alabama	No	No	No[1]
Alaska	Yes	Yes	Yes
Arizona	Yes	No	Yes
Arkansas	Yes[2]	Yes[2]	No
California	Yes	Yes	Yes
Colorado	Yes	Yes	Yes
Connecticut	Yes	Yes	Yes
Delaware	No	No	No[3]
Dist. of Columbia	No	No	Yes
Florida	Yes	Yes	No[4]
Georgia	Yes	Yes	Yes
Hawaii	Yes	Yes	Yes
Idaho	No	No	Yes
Illinois	No[3]	Yes	Yes
Indiana	Yes	Yes	Yes
Iowa	No	No	No
Kansas	No	No	No[5]
Kentucky	No	No	Yes
Louisiana	Yes	Yes	No[3]
Maine	No[6]	Yes	No

State	Physician	Hospital	Mental Health Records
Maryland	Yes	Yes	Yes
Massachusetts	No[6]	Yes	No[3]
Michigan	Yes	Yes	Yes
Minnesota	Yes	Yes	Yes
Mississippi	No	No[7]	Yes
Missouri	Yes	No	No[3]
Montana	Yes	Yes	Yes
Nebraska	No	Yes	No[8]
Nevada	Yes	Yes	Yes
New Hampshire	Yes	Yes	Yes
New Jersey	Yes	Yes	No[3]
New Mexico	No	No	No
New York	Yes	Yes	Yes
North Carolina	No	No	No[9]
North Dakota	No	No	No[3]
Ohio	No	Yes	Yes
Oklahoma	Yes	Yes	No[10]
Oregon	No[11]	No[11]	Yes
Pennsylvania	No	Yes	No
Rhode Island	No	No	No
South Carolina	Yes	No	Yes
South Dakota	Yes	Yes	Yes
Tennessee	No	No[7]	No[3]
Texas	No[6]	No[6]	Yes
Utah	No[3]	No[3]	No
Vermont	No	No	No
Virginia	Yes	Yes	Yes
Washington	Yes	Yes	Yes
West Virginia	Yes	Yes	No[3]
Wisconsin	Yes	Yes	Yes
Wyoming	No	Yes	No

NOTES

1. Records may be released by a court order only.
2. Records may be released to the subject-patient if a lawsuit is being prepared or has been filed.

3. Records will be released to the subject's attorney only.

4. The physician may provide a summary report of the record in lieu of the record itself.

5. Records may be released to patients in community or state mental health institutions.

6. The physician is required to provide either a summary of the record or the record itself.

7. "Good cause" must be demonstrated by a patient in order to obtain his or her record.

8. Records can be released to patients in state mental institutions.

9. Access is permitted to any individual who is or has been a patient of a mental health, substance abuse, or developmental disability treatment center.

10. Records may be released by court order or with consent of the treating physician(s).

11. State, community, or other nonprivate institutions are required to release records. Private institutions and physicians are not required, but are encouraged to do so.

Source: Diann Johnson and Sidney M. Wolfe. *Medical Records: Getting Yours.* Washington, D.C.: Public Citizen's Health Research Group, 1995. Used with permission.

Appendix III

List of Documents in a Medical Record

A. ADMINISTRATIVE RECORDS

1. Face Sheet
   Essential patient information, including name, address, telephone number, next-of-kin, religion, insurance coverage, and other data
2. Preadmission
   Prehospitalization care records, reports, approvals—including physician's office records—and any clinic records
3. Conditions of admission
   A statement indicating that the patient consents to receive basic, routine care and that the institution does not guarantee the outcome (usually shown on the reverse side of admission/discharge form)
4. Consent for routine procedures
   The form that is signed by the patient or an authorized representative at the time of admission
5. Special consents
   Informed consent, e.g. required for any nonroutine diagnostic or therapeutic procedure
6. Authorization for release of information
   Permits the hospital to allow access to the MR to specifically named organizations, for example, Blue Cross/Blue Shield, Medicare/Medicaid, HMOs, insurance companies
7. Attestation statement
   Required by Medicare. Certifies that the diagnoses and procedures performed are accurately and completely documented in the MR

B. CLINICAL RECORDS

1. Medical/physician
   a. History and physical (H&P)
      1. Physical examination (PE)—provides baseline data to assist in a diagnosis, includes a review of systems (ROS) and signs observed
      2. Past medical history (PMH)—may be used to establish a tentative/provisional diagnosis
      3. Family history including relatives with similar medical history and/or causes of death
      4. Social history—personal lifestyle, habits
      5. Details of patient's current chief complaint (symptoms)
      6. Statement of findings (diagnosis)
      7. Proposed plan of treatment
   b. Physicians' orders: These are written instructions to nursing and ancillary services and other physicians regarding all medications and treatments. Their purpose is to communicate the plan of care to all other members of the health care team. These orders include:
      1. Admission,
      2. Ongoing,
      3. Pre-and postoperative, and
      4. Discharge.
   c. Physicians' progress notes: These are a daily chronological narrative relating to the patient's diagnosis, course of treatment, response to the medical regimen, and the patient's ongoing status, up to and including discharge. These should include the patient's subjective statements (symptoms).
2. Nursing
   a. Admission history and physical assessment
   b. Nursing care plans, including *nursing* orders based on *nursing* diagnoses (may or may not be in record)
   c. Flow sheets, various check lists, graphic sheets
   d. Medication administration records (MAR)
   e. Miscellaneous nursing reports, for example, flow sheets in specialty units such as ICU and CCU
   f. Nurses' progress notes: These will be the most detailed progress notes. They describe the "nursing process"—all care given by nursing staff. They should confirm the implementation of physicians' orders. They will detail nursing assessments including the patient's physical and emotional state.
3. Laboratory reports

4. Pathology reports
5. Reports of other diagnostic tests and procedures
6. Radiology/nuclear medicine reports
    a. X-ray
    b. CAT
    c. MRI
7. Other studies
    a. EEG
    b. EKG
8. Consultation reports
9. Surgery/Operative reports
    a. Preoperative findings/diagnosis
    b. Operating room notes—surgeons', nurses'
    c. Surgeons participating—status of each
    c. Description of the surgical procedure
    d. Anesthesia
    e. Recovery room (PACU)
    f. Postoperative findings
    g. Any specimens removed for biopsy/testing
    h. Postoperative report, findings, diagnosis, prognosis
10. Ancillary caregiver/special disciplines
    a. Physical therapy
    b. Occupational therapy
    c. Respiratory therapy
    d. Social services
    e. Nutritionists
    f. Chaplains
11. Discharge summary and discharge planning and teaching
    a. Discharge summary of all treatment during hospital stay
    b. An evaluation of the patient's response to treatment
    c. Confirms physicians' final diagnosis
    d. Outlines the discharge plan—follow-up care regimen
    e. A statement of the patient's condition at time of discharge
12. Special clinical records
    a. Emergency transport: EMT, paramedic, ambulance any other other rescue personnel—will describe the patient's condition at the time of admission to the emergency room
    b. Emergency room

c. Coronary care
d. Intensive care
e. Dialysis
f. Psychiatry
g. Obstetrics
h. Neonatal—pre and postpartum
i. Post-discharge treatment records
j. Rehabilitation

C. MISCELLANEOUS RECORDS

a. Staff physicians' office records
b. Correspondence
c. Itemized billing statements
d. Referrals
e. Autopsy report

Appendix IV

Abbreviations Commonly Used in Medical and Nursing Clinical Practice

AUTHOR'S NOTE

Periods have been omitted from the list of abbreviations because in the clinical setting there is usually no consistent, standardized way of punctuating many of them. This will vary according to the individual practitioner's habit or an institution's approved list. The use of capital letters in abbreviations also varies. An authoritative medical dictionary should be consulted to confirm whether or not an abbreviation as written in the medical record is acceptable.

a	ante, before (usually written with a dash above the letter)
A & P	auscultation and percussion; anterior and posterior
A & W	alive and well
aa	of each
AAL	anterior axillary line
AB, ab	abortion
ABC	aspiration needle biopsy
abd	abdominal
ABG	arterial blood gas
ac	before meals; air conduction
accom	accommodation
AD	right ear
adeno-Ca	adenocarcinoma
ADH	antidiuretic hormone
ADL	activities of daily living

ad lib	at liberty; as desired; as tolerated
ADM	adult onset diabetes mellitus
AE	above the elbow
AGN	acute glomerulonephritis
AHF	antihemophilic factor
AI	aortic insufficiency
AIDS	acquired immune deficiency syndrome
AK	above the knee (amputation)
ALL	acute lymphocytic leukemia
am	morning, in the morning
AMA	against medical advice
AMI	acute myocardial infarction
AML	acute myelocytic leukemia
anes	anesthesia
ANS	autonomic nervous system
A-P	anterior-posterior
AP	anteroposterior
APVOD	arteriosclerotic peripheral vascular occlusive disease
aq	water
ARC	AIDS related complex
ARDS	adult respiratory distress syndrome
AS	left ear; arteriosclerosis; aortic stenosis
ASA	acetylsalycylic acid (aspirin)
ASAP	as soon as possible
ASD	atrial septal defect
astigm	astigmatism
ATN	acute tubular necrosis
AU	both ears
ausc	auscultation
AV	atriovenous; atrioventricular
AVR	aortic valve replacement
B	black
BA	barium
baso	basophil
BBB	bundle branch block
BC	bone conduction
BCP	birth control pill

BE	barium enema
BF	black female
bid	twice a day
bilat	bilateral
bin	twice during the night
BK	below the knee (amputation)
BM	bowel movement; black male
BMR	basal metabolic rate
BNO	bladder neck obstruction
BP	blood pressure
BPH	benign prostatic hypertrophy
BRP	bathroom privileges
BS	bowel sounds; blood sugar
BSC	bedside commode
BSE	breast self-exam
BT	bleeding time
BUN	blood, urea, nitrogen
BW	birthweight
BX, biop	biopsy
c	with (usually written with a dash above the letter)
C	centigrade; Celsius
C & S	culture and sensitivity
C-1, C-2	first cervical vertebra, second cervical vertebra
C-section	cesarean section
Ca	calcium
CA	cancer; carcinoma
CA	chronologic age
CAD	coronary artery disease
cap	capsule
CAPD	continuous ambulatory peritoneal dialysis
CAT	computerized axial tomography
cath	catheter
CBC, cbc	complete blood count
cc	cubic centimeter
CC	chief complaint
CCU	coronary/cardiac care unit
cervical dil	cervical dilation

ch br syn	chronic brain syndrome
CHD	congenital hip dislocation
CHF	congestive heart failure
chr	chronic
circ	circumcision; circulation
CK	creatine kinase
CLL	chronic lymphocytic leukemia
cm	centimeter
CML	chronic myelogenous leukemia
CNS	central nervous system
CO, c/o	complains of
CO_2	carbon dioxide
COAD	chronic obstructive airway disease
COLD	chronic obstructive lung disease
cong fail	congestive failure
COPD	chronic obstructive pulmonary disease
CP	cerebral palsy
CPD	cephalopelvic disproportion
CPK	creatinine phosphokinase
CPR	cardiopulmonary resuscitation
CRF	chronic renal failure
cs	cesarean section
CSF	cerebrospinal fluid
CT	computerized tomography
ct	count
cu	cubic
CV	cardiovascular
CVA	cerebrovascular accident
CVD	cerebrovascular disease
CVS	cardiovascular system
cx	cervix
CXR	chest x-ray
cysto	cystoscopic (examination)
d	day
D&C	dilatation and curettage
D&E	dilatation and evacuation
DAT	diet as tolerated

DC	discharge; discontinue
DC'd	discontinued
DDD	degenerative disk disease
derm	dermatology
DI	diabetes insipidus
diag	diagnosis; diagnostic
disc	discontinue
disch	discharge
diff	differential blood count
DJD	degenerative joint disease
DM	diabetes mellitus
DNR	do not resusciate
DOA	dead on arrival
DOB	date of birth
DOE	dyspnea on exertion
DPT	diptheria, pertussis, tetanus
DT	delirium tremens
DTR	deep tendon reflex
DUB	dysfunctional uterine bleeding
DVT	deep vein thrombosis
DX, Dx	diagnosis
EBV	Epstein-Barr virus
ECC	extracorporeal circulation
ECF	extracellular fluid; extended care facility
ECG	electrocardiogram
EDC	estimated, expected, date of confinement
EEG	electroencephalogram
EENT	ears, eyes, nose, and throat
EKG	electrocardiogram
EMG	electromyogram
ENT	ears, nose, and throat
EOM	extraocular movement
eos, eosin	eosinophil
ER	emergency room
ESR	erythrocyte sedimentation rate
et	and
etiol	etiology

EUA	exam under anesthesia
exc	excision
ext	extremity
F	female; fahrenheit
FB, fb	foreign body
FBS	fasting blood sugar
Fe	iron
FEF	forced expiratory flow
FEKG	fetal electrocardiogram
FEV	forced expiratory volume
FH	family history
FHR	fetal heart rate
FHS	fetal heart sounds
FHT	fetal heart tones
FS	frozen section
FTND	full-term normal delivery
F/U, FU	follow-up
FUO	fever of undetermined origin
FVC	forced vital capacity
FX, fx	fracture
GB	gallbladder
GBS	gallbladder series
GFR	glomerular filtration rate
GH	growth hormone
GI	gastrointestinal
GM, gm	gram
gm neg	gram negative
gr	grain
GRAV, grav	gravida (a pregnant woman)
gtt	drop
GTT	glucose tolerance test
GU	genitourinary
GYN, gyn	gynecology
h	hour
H	hydrogen
H&E	hemorrhage and exudate

H&P	history and physical
H_2O	water
H_2O_2	hydrogen peroxide
HBP	high blood pressure
HCT, hct	hematocrit
HCVD	hypertensive cardiovascular disease
HD	hemodialysis
HDL	high density lipoprotien
HEENT	head, ears, eyes, nose, and throat
Hg	mercury
HGB, hgb	hemoglobin
HGH	human growth hormone
H-J	hepatojugular
HNP	herniated nucleus pulposus
H/O	history of
HOB	head of bed
HPI	history of present illness
HR	heart rate
HS, hs	hour of sleep; at bedtime
HT, HTN	hypertension
HVD	hypertensive vascular disease
HX	history
hypo	hypodermic
I&D	incision and drainage
I&O	intake and output (fluids, drainage)
ICF	intermediate care facility
ICU	intensive care unit
ID	intradermal
IDDM	insulin dependent diabetes mellitus
IH	infectious hepatitis
IM	intramuscular
IMP, imp	impression
inf	infusion; inferior
inj	injection
int	internal
IOP	intraocular pressure

IPP & A	inspection, percussion, palpation and auscultation
IPPB	intermittent positive pressure breathing
IS	intercostal space; incentive spirometry
ITP	idiopathic thrombocytopenic purpura
IU	international unit; immunizing unit
IUD	intrauterine device
IV	intravenous
IVP	intravenous pyelogram
IVSD	interventricular septal defect
JV	jugulovenous
JVP	jugulovenous pulse
K	potassium
KCl	potassium chloride
KD	knee disarticulation
kg	kilogram
KJ	knee-jerk
KUB	kidneys, ureters, bladder
KVO	keep vein open
L	left (the letter is usually circled in this usage)
L&A	light and accomodation
L&D	labor and delivery
L&W	living and well
L, l	liter
L-1, L-2	first lumbar vertebra, second lumbar vertebra
lap	laparotomy
lat	lateral
lb	pound
LB	large bowel
LBBB	left bundle branch block
LCM	left costal margin
LDL	low density lipoprotein
LE	left eye; lower extremity
LE	lupus erythematosis
LFT	liver function tests
LLE	left lower extremity
LLL	left lower lobe
LLQ	left lower quadrant

LMD	left midline deviation
LMP	last menstrual period
LN	lymph node
LOA	left occipitoanterior
LOC	loss of consciousness; level of care
LOS	length of stay
LOT	left occiput transverse
LP	lumbar puncture
LRQ	lower right quadrant
LSK	liver, spleen, kidney
lt	left
ltd	limited
LUE	left upper extremity
LUL	left upper lobe
LUQ	left upper quadrant
LV	left ventricle
LVH	left ventricular hypertrophy
lymph	lymphocyte
M	male; meter
MA	mental age
MBC	maximum breathing capacity
mcg	microgram
MCL	midclavicular line
MD	muscular dystrophy
meds	medications
mEq	milliequivalent
mEq/L	milliequivalents per liter
mets	metastasis; metastases
mg	milligram
Mg	magnesium
MGF	maternal grandfather
MGGM	maternal great grandfather
MH	marital history; mental health
MI	myocardial infarction; mitral insufficiency
ml	milliliter
mm	millimeter
mm Hg	millimeters of mercury

MOM	milk of magnesia
mono	monocyte
MRI	magnetic resonance imaging
MS	mitral stenosis; multiple sclerosis
MSL	midsternal line
MSU	midstream urine (catch)
MTD	right ear drum
MTS	left ear drum
MVP	mitral valve prolapse
MVR	mitral valve replacement
MVV	maximum voluntary ventilation
myop	myopia
N	nitrogen
N&V	nausea and vomiting
Na	sodium
NaCl	sodium chloride
NAD	no acute distress
NB	newborn
NBS	normal breath sounds
NED	no evidence of disease
neg	negative
NER	no evidence of recurrence
NERD	no evidence of recurrent disease
NG	nasogastric
NH	nursing home; neurologic history
NIDDM	noninsulin dependent diabetes mellitus
NKA	no known allergies
NMR	nuclear magnetic resonance
non rep	do not repeat
NOS	not otherwise specified
NPO	nothing by mouth
NSAID	nonsteroidal anti-inflammatory drug
NSR	normal sinus rhythm
NSVD	normal spontaneous vaginal delivery
NTP	normal temperature and pressure
O & P	ova and parasites
O_2	oxygen

OA	osteoarthritis
OB	obstetrics
OBS	organic brain syndrome
OC	oral contraceptive
occ	occasional
OD	right eye; overdose; once a day
OHS	open heart surgery
OOB	out of bed
OP	occiput posterior
OPD	outpatient department
ophth	ophthalmology
OR	operating room
ORTH, ortho	orthopedics
os	mouth
OS	left eye
OT	occupational therapy
oto	otology
OU	both eyes
OV	each eye
oz	ounce
p	post; after (usually written with a dash above the letter)
P	pulse, para
P & A	percussion and auscultation
P-A	posterior-anterior
PA	posteroanterior; pernicious anemia
PAC	premature atrial contraction
$PaCO_2$	pressure of carbon dioxide
PACU	postanesthesia care unit
PaO_2	pressure of oxygen
PAP	Papanicolaou (smear/test)
para	number of pregnancies
pares	paresthesia
PAT	paroxysmal atrial tachycardia
path	pathology
pc	after meals
PCN	penicillin
PCO_2	pressure of carbon dioxide

PCV	packed cell volume
PD	peritoneal dialysis
PDA	patent ductus arteriosus
PE	physical examination
peds	pediatrics
PEG	pneumoencephalogram
PERLA	pupils equal and react to light and accomodation
PERRLA	pupils equal, round, and reactive to light and accommodation
PET	positron emission tomography
PE tube	perieustachian tube
PFT	pulmonary function test
PGF	paternal grandfather
PGH	pituitary growth hormone
pH	hydrogen ion concentration (degree of acidity)
PH	past history
PI	present illness
PID	pelvic inflammatory disease
PKU	phenylketonuria
PM	postmortem; petit mal (seizure)
pm, PM	afternoon, in the afternoon
PMH	past medical history
PMP	previous menstrual period
PND	paroxysmal nocturnal dyspnea
PNS	peripheral nervous system
PO	postoperative; by mouth
PO_2	pressure of oxygen
pp	after meals; postpartum
preop	preoperative
PRN, prn	as necessary
PROM	passive range of motion; premature rupture of membranes
prot	protocol
pro-time	prothrombin time
pt	pint
PT	patient; physical therapy; prothrombin time
PTA	prior to admission
PTH	parathyroid hormone
PTT	partial thromboplastin time

PU	pregnancy urine
PVC	premature ventricular contraction
q	each; every
qam	every morning
qd	every day
qh	every hour
q_h	every_hours
qhs	every hour of sleep; at bedtime
qid	four times during the day
qn	every night
qod	every other day
qs	in a quantity sufficient
QS	every shift
qt	quart
R	right (the letter is usually circled in this usage); respirations
RA	rheumatoid arthritis; right atrium
RATX	radiation therapy
RBBR	right bundle branch block
RBC	red blood cell; red blood cell count
RCM	right costal margin
RD	respiratory disease
RDA	recommended dietary allowance
RDS	respiratory distress syndrome
RE	right eye
REM	rapid eye movement
RF	rheumatoid factor
Rh	Rhesus (monkey) blood factor—(+ or −)
RHD	rheumatic heart disease
RLE	right lower extremity
RLL	right lower lobe
RLQ	right lower quadrant
RML	right middle lobe
RNA	ribonucleic acid
RO	rule out
ROA	right occiput anterior
ROM	range of motion
ROP	right occiput posterior

ROS	review of systems
ROT	right occiput transverse
RP	retrograde pyelogram
RR	recovery room; respiratory rate
rt	right
RT	radiation therapy
RUA	routine urine analysis
RUE	right upper extremity
RUL	right upper lobe
RUQ	right upper quadrant
RV	right ventricle
Rx	treatment; therapy; take
s	without (usually written with a dash above the letter)
S-1, S-2	first sacral vertebra, second sacral vertebra
SA	sinoatrial (node)
SBE	shortness of breath on exertion
SC, sc	subcutaneously
SCD	sudden cardiac death
SD	shoulder disarticulation
sed rate	sedimentation rate
SGOT	serum glutamic oxaloacetic transaminase
SGPT	serum glutamic pyruvic transaminase
SH	social history; serum hepatitis
SIDS	sudden infant death syndrome
SLE	systemic lupus erythematosus
SLR	straight leg raising
SOB	short of breath
sol	solution
sos	if necessary
SP	status post
sp gr	specific gravity
sq	squamous
SR	sedimentation rate
ss	one half
SS, S & S	signs and symptoms
SSE	soap suds enema
ss gl	without glasses (or corrective lenses)

staph	Staphylococcus, a genus of micrococci
stat	immediately
STD	sexually transmitted disease
strep	Streptococcus, a genus of bacteria
STS	serological test for syphillis
STSG	split thickness skin graft
subc, subq	subcutaneous
suppos	suppository
surg	surgical
SVC	superior vena cava
SX	symptom
T	temperature
T & A	tonsillectomy and adenoidectomy
T-1, T-2	first thoracic vertebra, second thoracic vertebra
tab	tablet
tachy	tachycardia
TAH	total abdominal hysterectomy
TAT	tetanus antitoxin
TB	tuberculosis
TBA	to be admitted
TBI	total body irradiation
TC & DB	turn, cough, and deep breathing
temp	temperature
THA	total hip arthroplasty
THR	total hip replacement
TIA	transient ischemic attack
tid	three times a day
TKA	total knee arthroplasty
TKR	total knee replacement
TL	tubal ligation
TM	tympanic membrane
TO	telephone order
top	topically
TPN	total parenteral nutrition
TPR	temperature, pulse and respirations
TPUR	transperineal urethral resection
TSH	thyroid stimulating hormone

TUR	transurethral resection
TURP	transurethral resection of the prostate; transurethral prostatectomy
TV	total volume
TX	treatment; traction
U, u	unit
UA	urine analysis
UC	uterine contractions
UCHD	usual childhood diseases
UGI	upper gastrointestinal
ULQ	upper left quadrant
umb	umbilicus; navel
ung	ointment
ur	urine
URI	upper respiratory infection
urol	urology
URQ	upper right quadrant
US	ultrasound
UTI	urinary tract infection
UV	ultraviolet
VA	visual acuity
VBG	venous blood gas
VC	vital capacity
VD	veneral disease
VF	visual field; field of vision
VHD	ventricular heart disease
VO	verbal order
VS	vital signs
VSD	ventricular septal defect
VV	varicose vein
WBC, wbc	white blood cell; white blood cell count
WC	wheel chair
WD	well-developed
WDWN	well-developed, well-nourished
WF	white female
wk	week
WM	white male

WN	well-nourished
WNL	within normal limits
WO	without
wt	weight
XX	female sex chromosome
XY	male sex chromosome
YO, y/o	year-old

Glossary

abandonment: The abrupt, unjustified, dissolution by a health care provider of duty to a patient without the patient's consent or foreknowledge.

absolute privilege: The protection, granted under law, to the confidentiality of communications between an attorney and the attorney's client.

action: Lawsuit.

administrative agency: A department of government that promulgates, administers, and enforces the statutory laws enacted by that government.

administrative laws: Those rules and regulations created and enforced by administrative agencies in order to enforce statutory laws.

admissions of fact: Written requests by both sides asking each other to admit to, or deny, certain facts concerning the issues presented in a lawsuit.

advance directive: A written, signed, legal document that defines a competent individual's wishes regarding life-sustaining medical intervention on their behalf in the event that they would become incompetent.

affidavit: A declaration or written statement of facts made voluntarily and while under an oath administered by an officer of a court or by a notary.

affirmative defense: A challenge by the defendant to the plaintiff's legal right to bring a lawsuit rather than a challenge to the veracity of the plaintiff's claims.

amended pleadings: Those that in some way alter pleadings previously entered in the lawsuit.

assault: Any attempt or threat made by one person to use force upon, to inflict injury upon, or to touch another person in an offensive way without his or her consent. It is any willful action or statement that creates fear or apprehension of being touched in an injurious or abhorrent manner. Actual touching need not occur. A threatened battery.

battery: The intentional, unpermitted, and wrongful touching of another person, or that person's possessions, in an injurious or offensive manner.

borrowed servant doctrine: The temporary assignment of vicarious liability from a principal employer to a designated employer who then becomes legally responsible for any employee who, voluntarily, is "borrowed" from his primary employer.

breach of duty: Any failure in a defined legal, moral, or ethical duty owed. Negligence in the proper performance or fulfillment of the duties inherent in a position, office, or profession.

burden of proof: "*Onus probandi*": Under the laws of evidence, this is the requirement that either party in a lawsuit is obligated to prove, by a preponderance of evidence, the allegations that they make. This burden usually falls upon the plaintiff.

capacity: The intellectual capability to understand the nature, the purpose, and the consequences of ones actions.

captain of the ship doctrine: The physician in charge is responsible for the actions of those staff assigned to assist him or her for the duration of a medical or surgical procedure.

causation: Any antecedent action or situation that can define a consequent effect.

cause in fact: The specific action or situation that defines a consequent effect without which the effect could not have come about.

cause of action: Those alleged facts that give an individual sufficient legal right to initiate a claim in law for redress, relief, or other form of judicial remedy in his or her own behalf.

caveat: lit.: "beware" or "take heed." A caution or warning. *Caveat emptor*: "Let the buyer beware." *Caveat lector*: "Let the reader beware."

civil law: The body of law that addresses noncriminal litigation, for example, the rights and duties of parties involved in contracts, torts, and patents.

civil penalty: Monetary compensation (damages) or other form of retribution prescribed and imposed as a penalty for violation of a civil law.

claims-made policy: That form of a malpractice insurance policy that provides coverage only for claims made and reported to the insurer, during the period in which the policy is in effect or during the "tail."

comparative negligence: The degree of relative negligence and liability is measured in proportion to the percentage of shared fault for or relative contribution to the plaintiff's injuries on the part of the plaintiff and/or one or more defendants. Damages claimed are then apportioned accordingly as determined by the jury.

compensatory damages: An amount awarded to an injured party to compensate for the injury by indemnification for any loss caused by the injury.

competency: Legal capacity. An affirmation of competency may be sought from and declared by a court.

complaint: The document in which the plaintiff, under oath, presents allegations of injury and a formal plea to a civil court for relief under the law in a claim for damages. Also called a petition. It is a statement of cause for judicial action against a named defendant.

consent: A voluntary acquiescence, approval, agreement, or permission conveyed by one person to another that allows the other to do something to or for the person consenting.

contributory negligence: A negligent action or omission on the part of a plaintiff that, together with a like action or omission on the part of a defendant, constitutes a proximate cause of the injuries claimed by the plaintiff.

corporate negligence: Legal principle under which a corporate entity is held liable for the actions or omissions of employees while those employees are on the job and acting within the scope of their job descriptions.

counterclaim: A claim made by a defendant that disputes, denies, opposes, contradicts, or refutes the claims made by the plaintiff and that attempts to show cause for action in favor of the defendant.

damage: The injury, harm, or loss sustained by one person as a result of the tortious action of another.

damages: The amount of money claimed and/or awarded as compensation for damage.

defamation: The intentional publication of false information that injures the reputation of another. Includes slander and libel.

default judgment: Made by the court in favor of a plaintiff when a defendant fails to respond to a lawsuit or to appear at the trial in his own defense.

defendant: The accused; the person or entity that is sued. The one against whom a lawsuit is brought and who is charged with defending against the allegations and the claims of the plaintiff for relief under the law.

defense: That which is offered and alleged by the defendant in response to the action or suit by a plaintiff and attempts to show as a reason in law or in fact why the plaintiff should not recover damages.

deponent: The individual who is called upon to testify under oath to the truth of certain facts presented orally or in writing.

deposition: The procedure of deriving pretrial testimony from a deponent.

discovery: The pretrial procedures and methods used to obtain all relevant information from opposing parties in a lawsuit.

discovery rule: Under this rule, the statue of limitations in malpractice does not commence until the actual date of discovery of the malpractice by the plaintiff or that date on which any reasonable person could have or should have discovered that an injury was the result of malpractice.

dual servant doctrine: The legal concept that recognizes shared liability on the part of both a principal and a secondary employer for the actions of a shared employee.

durable power of attorney: A form of an advance directive that appoints another to act as proxy decision maker should the grantor become incompetent. Revokable; it is nullified when the grantor dies.

duty: A legal or moral obligation owed by one person to another to conform to defined, acceptable standards of conduct in order to protect others from unreasonable risks.

emancipated minor: Any individual under the legal age of majority who is totally self-supporting and no longer under the control of or dependent on the care of a parent or guardian.

exclusions: The provisions in any insurance policy that define the conditions, occurrences, or circumstances that are not covered under the terms of the policy.

expert witness: An individual who, by reason of specialized education, training, and experience, possesses a superior degree of knowledge regarding specific subjects that, ordinarily, another person would not possess.

fact witness: An individual who has direct knowledge of and testifies to the factual circumstances and issues involved in a lawsuit. A material witness.

false imprisonment: The unlawful, unjustified, and intentional restraint, detention, or confinement of a person without his or her consent and/or without legal warrant, so that the person so confined is conscious of the confinement and threatened or harmed by it.

foreseeability: The perception and understanding, expected of any reasonable and prudent person, of the liability for and the consequences of their actions or omissions—particularly regarding the inherent risks to others.

general damages: Monetary compensation awarded to a plaintiff for pain, suffering, and other abstract injuries caused by the negligence of a defendant.

gross negligence: The willful failure to perform a manifest duty with reckless disregard for the possible or probable consequences of that failure regarding the well-being of another. It may be an action or an omission.

guardian-ad-litem: An individual appointed by a court to act as a special and impartial guardian to represent an unborn, an infant, a ward, or any person adjudicated as incompetent. The appointment exists only for the duration of the particular litigation involved.

guidelines: A defined or recommended course of action or series of procedures that, if followed, will enable effective implementation of a policy or attainment of a goal.

hard damages: Monetary compensation awarded to a plaintiff for the specific amounts of expenses and financial losses incurred and claimed to have resulted from the defendant's negligence.

hearsay evidence: That testimony of a witness who presents not what he or she knows directly and personally, but what he or she has heard or been told.

A statement made by someone other than the declarent that is offered as evidence, but not generally admissible.

incompetence: The lack of legal or professional qualifications, knowledge, ability, or suitability to discharge a duty. A determination of competency may be a matter for a court.

informed consent: Consent given only after a full disclosure and confirmed understanding of all pertinent facts necessary for the individual to make an intelligent, reasonable, and voluntary choice.

intent: The desire, design, determination, or resolve with which a person acts to accomplish a given purpose through a deliberate course of action.

intentional infliction of emotional distress: The egregious and willful invasion of another's peace of mind in a manner that is wanton, outrageous, and beyond all acceptable standards of decency and morality.

intentional tort: A civil wrong resulting from an intentional act by the tortfeasor, that causes injury or harm to another's person or property.

interrogatories: A pretrial discovery procedure in which a series of written questions are presented to the opposing parties named in the lawsuit. The answers are presented under oath.

invasion of privacy: The unwarranted publication of another person's private affairs or the intrusion into another's private activities in such a way as to violate their intrinsic rights and cause them personal harm in some way.

judgment: The adjudicated decision of a court that defines the rights and duties of the parties in a lawsuit.

judicial law: Rules of law established by courts or the judiciary. Decisional law.

jury: "Twelve persons selected to decide who has the best lawyer." (Robert Frost)

law: That which is laid down and established as the embodiment of those rules of conduct defined by a legal authority and having binding legal force on the members of a society.

lay witness: An individual who is called upon to give testimony on matters regarding the lawsuit, but who possesses no special knowledge or expertise regarding the issues or facts about which he or she testifies.

liability: Legal duty, responsibility, or obligation each person is bound to in law or justice to perform. Legal accountability and responsibility for one's personal actions or conduct.

libel: Defamation that is expressed in writing or pictorially.

licensure: The procedures by which an agency of government coveys the right, permission, and authority to a person or entity to engage legally in an activity, practice, or professional occupation.

living will: A form of advance directive. A written, signed, and witnessed legal document that defines a person's wishes regarding life-sustaining measures of medical intervention to be implemented on his or her behalf in the event that the person becomes incompetent.

locality rule: Refers to those standards of care that prevail in a community or a defined geographical area. National standards have largely displaced these in malpractice lawsuits.

malice: The state of mind that motivates an individual to willfully commit a wrongful act with the deliberate intent to injure another or with wanton disregard of the likelihood of such injury as a consequence of his or her action.

malpractice: Negligence or misconduct on the part of a professional while acting in the capacity of a professional. A failure in professional duties or standards that causes harm or injury to another.

mandatory licensure: A statutory requirement which permits the practice of certain professions or activities only to those who have received a license to engage legally in such practice.

material risk: An apparent and significant danger that any reasonable person should recognize as a likely consequence of an action or omission.

motion: A formal application made to a court in order to obtain a ruling or order that directs an action in favor of the applicant.

motion for a directed verdict: A formal request that a lawsuit be concluded by a verdict in favor of the defendant because the plaintiff has not met the burden of proof or the defendant has presented a sufficient, irrefutable defense.

motion to dismiss: Application to the court requesting that the court set aside the case because there is no valid cause of action or form of relief.

negligence: Ordinary negligence. The failure to act with that degree of care that any ordinary, prudent, and reasonable person would exercise in the same or similar circumstances.

non compos mentis: lit.: not of sound mind. Incompetent, insane, afflicted with some form of debilitating mental impairment.

nonmaleficence: The legal and moral principle that enjoins health care providers to do no harm to a patient—intentionally or otherwise.

nonsuit: The adverse judgment of the court when the plaintiff fails to properly proceed to a trial leaving the allegations unresolved or is unable to sustain the burden of proof during a trial. Also used to indicate a defendant who is discharged from a lawsuit.

occurrence-basis, occurrence policy: The category of professional liability insurance that protects the insured for acts of malpractice that occur while the policy is in effect, regardless of when a claim is made afterward.

ordinary negligence: (*See* negligence.)

ostensible authority: The doctrine of law whereby an institution is liable for the negligence of an independent contractor if a patient has a reasonable basis to assume that such a contractor is an employee of the institution.

parens patriae: lit.: parent of the nation. Refers to the role of the state in its sovereign capacity as legal guardian of an adjudicated incompetent person, or a person having some form of legal disability that prevents their acting on their own behalf.

party: A person or entity that is designated in a lawsuit as either a plaintiff or a defendant of record.

personal liability: The legal and moral doctrine that holds the individual solely responsible and fully accountable for his or her own actions or omissions.

petition: A formal written application to the court requesting judicial intervention in the matter presented and a presentation of allegations and facts that have given rise to the cause of action. (*See* complaint.)

plaintiff: The party who brings an action, who sues in a civil court, seeking damages or other form of relief under the law for alleged damage, loss, or harm caused by the defendant.

pleadings: The formal presentment to the court of claims and defenses by the respective parties in a lawsuit. A statement of the plaintiff's cause for action and the defendants defence and/or refutation of that cause.

precedent: A case that has been decided or adjudicated by a court and that is afterward accepted and cited as authoritative in the adjudication of a similar case or like matters or questions of law. Also known as the doctrine of *stare decisis*.

prima facie: lit.: at first sight, on primary appearance, on the face of it. A fact or matter that can be judged at its first disclosure and presumed to be true unless or until it can be proven untrue by evidence to the contrary.

privileged communication: The transmission of information or facts between or among those individuals who in a professional relationship are protected by law or custom from compelled divulgence of such confidences.

procedural law: That body of law that defines the processes, methods, and procedures to be used in enforcing legal rights and obtaining relief or redress when they are violated.

proximate cause: That continuous sequence of actions or natural happenings that, without any other identifiable intervening factors, produces an effect that, otherwise, would not have occurred.

prudent patient standard: Takes into consideration the principal risks and the likely consequences that would be apparent to, and understandable by, any reasonable, prudent person in a decision to accept or reject medical treatment.

punitive damages: Exemplary damages. Those that are awarded, in addition to ordinary or general damages, against a defendant as punishment for the egregious nature of the tort.

qualified privilege: Defense to a *prima faciae* case of defamation when it can be shown that there was no malicious intent on the part of the defendant. That is, the statements were made in duty or good faith, in a reasonable manner, for a valid reason, and directed to another person with a legitimate right to know.

question of fact: A disputed fact, claim, or issue that is usually left to the jury to decide and resolve.

question of law: A disputed legal contention that is usually left to the court, the judge, to decide. This involves the application or interpretation of the law itself and, therefore, is appropriately within the purview of the court rather than a jury.

release: A statement, written or oral, that declares the maker's intent to discharge another person from an existing or asserted duty, or the abandonment or relinquishment of a present and/or future claim or right.

requests for production of documents and things: A step in the discovery process. Formal requisition made by parties in a lawsuit to each side for any and all items that might provide discoverable facts pertinent to the issues.

res ipsa loquitur: lit.: "Let the thing speak for itself." The negligence of the defendant can be inferred or presumed, based on proof that the instrumentality that caused the plaintiff's injury was under the exclusive control of the defendant and that the injury is such that it otherwise could have not have occurred except in negligence.

respondeat superior: lit.: "Let the master answer." The master is responsible for the acts of the servant. An employer is indirectly liable, under certain circumstances, for the wrongful acts of an employee while the employee is acting within the course of employment. This includes negligence that causes harm or injury to another.

scope of practice: Those limits, duties, and responsibilities of any given profession that are defined by statutes, rules, and regulations.

service: Service of process, a summons. The delivery of an official notice to the defendant that a lawsuit, claim, or a charge has been filed against him or her.

settlement: The private agreement and transactions between the parties to a pending lawsuit to effect a resolution of all claims and issues involved.

slander: Oral defamation.

soft damages: Monetary compensation awarded to a plaintiff for such things as loss of consortium, pain and suffering, emotional distress, and disfigurement.

special damages: Damages based on the plaintiff's actual or anticipated, direct or indirect, monetary losses or expenses, which are directly attributable to the defendant's negligence.

standard: An established, authoritative, and generally accepted rule, model, or criterion that serves as a basis of evaluation, comparison, or validation.

standard of care: In tort law, that average, acceptable degree of skill, care, and diligence that a reasonable and prudent person in the same profession would, or should, exercise in the same or similar circumstances.

stare decisis: lit.: "Let the decision stand." (*See* precedent.)

statute of limitations: The procedural law that defines the maximum duration of time within which certain legal actions can be brought by a plaintiff.

substantive law: That body of law that creates, defines, directs, and controls individual rights and duties, and which identifies specific causes for action regarding such rights and duties.

substitute judgment: A subjective assessment or decision by one person as to how another person would decide, if that other person were, in fact, competent to do so.

supplemental pleadings: (*See* amended pleadings.)

tail: An uninterrupted extension of the coverage period of a malpractice insurance policy; also known as the extended reporting endorsement.

testimony: Statements of evidence given by a competent witness under oath.

therapeutic privilege: The legal concept that sanctions the withholding of information by a health care provider when such information is deemed likely to jeopardize the health and well-being of a patient.

tort: A civil wrong, other than that involved in a contract, which results from a breach of duty and which produces harm or injury to the person or property of another.

tortfeasor: One who commits a tort.

unintentional tort: A civil wrong resulting from an unintentional act by the tortfeasor that causes injury or harm to another's person or property.

vicarious liability: The imputing of liability on one person for the wrongful actions of another based on a direct relationship between the two persons. Also known as substituted liability.

voir dire: A judicial process. A requirement "to speak the truth."

waiver: Voluntary relinquishment of a right.

writ of *certiorari*: A formal written petition to the Supreme Court, made by the losing party, that the court review his or her case.

writ of *habeas corpus*: lit.: "You have the body." A legal procedure to determine the legality of an individual's custody or confinement by having the person brought before the court at his or her own request or on order of the court itself (the writ).

Bibliography

BOOKS

Aiken, Tonia, and Joseph Catalano. *Legal, Ethical, and Political Issues in Nursing.* F. A. Davis, 1994.

American Medical Association, Council on Ethical and Judicial Affairs. *Code of Medical Ethics: Current Opinions.* 1992.

Appleby, Kristyn S., and Joanne Tarver. *Medical Records Review.* 2d ed. *Cumulative Supplement.* John Wiley & Sons, Inc., 1997.

Appleby, Kristyn S., and Joanne Tarver. *Medical Records Review.* 2d ed. John Wiley & Sons, Inc., 1994.

Black, Henry C. *Black's Law Dictionary.* 6th ed. West Publishing, 1990.

Danelson, Stephanie A. *Medical Malpractice Guide for Paralegals.* John Wiley & Sons, Inc., 1995.

Fiesta, Janine. *20 Legal Pitfalls for Nurses to Avoid.* Delmar Publishers, 1994.

Goldberg, Alan S., and Jocelyn F. Gordon. *Telemedicine: Emerging Legal Issues.* American Health Lawyers Association, 1998.

Inlander, Charles B., and Eugene I. Pavalon. *Your Medical Rights.* People's Medical Society, 1994.

Johnson, Diann, and Sidney M. Wolfe. *Medical Records: Getting Yours.* Public Citizen's Health Research Group, 1995.

Joint Commission on Accreditation of Healthcare Organizations. *Comprehensive Accreditation Manual for Hospitals,* 1997.

Kaizer, Arleen M. *Medical Records and How They Affect Legal Issues.* Aegean Park Press, 1994.

Lewis, Randine A. *Techniques of Medical Litigation: A Professional's Handbook for Plaintiffs, Defendants, & Medical Consultants.* Greenwood Publishing Group, Inc., 1997.

McCord, James W. *The Litigation Paralegal: A Systems Approach*. West Publishing Co., 1992.

McQuade, J. Stanley. *Analyzing Medical Records: A Method for Trial Lawyers*. Harrison Co., 1996.

Miller, Roger, and Mary S. Urisko. *West's Paralegal Today*. West Publishing Co., 1996.

National Association of Legal Assistants. *NALA Manual for Legal Assistants*. 2d ed. West Publishing Co., 1991.

Privacy Protection Study Commission. *Record-keeping in the Medical-care Relationship: Personal Privacy in an Information Society*. U.S. Government Printing Office, 1977.

Richards, Edward P., and Katharine Rathbun. *Law and the Physician: A Practical Guide*. Little Brown and Co., 1993. (An electronic book, online—see list of Web sites.)

Richards, Edward P., and Katharine Rathbun. *Medical Risk Management: Preventive Legal Strategies for Health Care Providers*. Aspen Publishers, Inc., 1983. (An electronic book, online—see list of Web sites.)

Roach, William F. *Medical Records & the Law*. Aspen Publishers, Inc., 1994.

Scott, Ronald W. *Legal Aspects of Documenting Patient Care*. Aspen Publishers, Inc., 1994.

Sharpe, Charles C. *Nursing Malpractice: Liability and Risk Management*. Auburn House, 1999.

Tunno, David. *Taking the Stand: Tips for the Expert Witness*. Lawyers & Judges Publishing Co., 1995.

United States Department of Health and Human Services, Public Health Service, Health Resources and Service Administration, Bureau of Health Professions, Division of Quality Assurance. *National Practitioner Data Bank 1997 Annual Report*.

United States Department of Health and Human Services, Public Health Service, Health Resources and Service Administration. Bureau of Health Professions, Division of Quality Assurance. *National Practitioner Data Bank Guidebook*, 1996.

United States Departments of Commerce and Health and Human Services. *Telemedicine Report to Congress*, January 31, 1997. (The complete text of the report is available from: http://www.ntia.doc.gov/reports/telemed/index.htm.)

Wolfe, Sidney, Mary Gabay, Phyllis McCarthy, Alana Bame, and Benita Adler. *Questionable Doctors*. Public Citizen's Health Research Group, 1998.

ARTICLES

American Health Information Management Association. Issue: Patient anonymity. *Journal of the American Health Information Management Association* (November/December 1997). Practice brief insert. No author. Not paginated.

American Health Information Management Association. Issue: Retention of health information. *Journal of the American Health Information Management Association* (January 1997). Practice brief insert. No author. Not paginated

American Health Information Management Association. Issue: Disclosure of health information. *Journal of the American Health Information Management Association* (September 1996). Practice brief insert. No author. Not paginated.

American Health Information Management Association. Issue: Authentication of medical record entries. *Journal of the American Health Information Management Association* (August 1996). Practice Brief insert. No author. Not paginated.

Clark, Lana J. Analyzing medical records: Don't panic—it's easier than it looks. *Legal Assistant Today* (May/June 1993): 84–86.

Cournoyer, Carmelle P. 1995. How to protect yourself legally after a patient is injured. *Nursing95 Career Directory* (January): 18–23.

Danelson, Stephanie A. Medical records summaries and medical chronologies. *Legal Assistant Today* (May/June 1995): 76–77.

Danelson, Stephanie A. Settle or take it to court? The paralegal's role in preparing a case for settlement. *Legal Assistant Today* (May/June 1994): 90–92.

Danelson, Stephanie A. Winding your way through the medical research maze. *Legal Assistant Today* (May/June 1993): 118–120.

Danelson, Stephanie A. Making sense of medical records. *Legal Assistant Today* (May/June 1992): 64–68.

DeWitt, A. L. Unlocking the mysteries of medical records. *Legal Assistant Today* (July/August 1997): 60–67.

Dwight, J. The nuts & bolts of civil case organization. *Legal Assistant Today* (March/April 1995): 56–59.

Fiesta, Janine. 1994. Incident reports. Confidential or not? *Nursing Management* 25 (10): 17–18.

Fortin, Frank. Internet medicine from chat room to waiting room. *Professional Medical Assistant* (January/February 1998): 18–20.

Gobis, Linda J. 1996. Telenursing: Nursing by telephone across state lines. *Journal of Nursing Law* 3 (3) (March): 7–17.

Goodman, Ellen. Courts need neutral experts to separate science from fiction. *The Morning Call* (February 24, 1998): A11.

Hart, Linda J. Alterations to medical records can be detected. *Professional Medical Assistant* (November/December 1994): 19–20.

Hunt, Stacy. Organized chaos: Making medical records make sense. *Legal Assistant Today* (November/December 1996): 68–69.

Jeffrey, Nancy Ann. Getting access to your medical records may be limited, costly—or impossible. *Wall Street Journal* (July 31, 1996): C1.

Jury Verdict Review Publications. *Pennsylvania Jury Verdicts.* (October 4, 1993): 17.

Kjervik, D. K. 1997. Telenursing—licensure and communication challenges. *Journal of Professional Nursing* 13 (2) (March–April): 65.

Leiter, Richard A., and Kathleen Miller. Medical research: And you thought legalese was hard to understand. *Legal Assistant Today* (July/August 1993): 124–127.

Lobb, Michael L., Gary C. Riley, and April M. Clemens. The legal nurse consultant's role on the defense team in a medical malpractice lawsuit. *Network* 5 (4) (April 1994): 3–7.

Mason, Marilyn. Finding the needle in the medical records haystack. *Legal Assistant Today* (September/October 1993): 82–89.

Miller, Carol. There's an attorney here to see you. *Professional Medical Assistant* (September/October 1996): 13–14.

Pear, Robert. Measure would protect medical record privacy. *San Francisco Examiner* (August 10, 1997): A-4.

Samuels, Bruce, and Sydney Wolfe. How to obtain your medical records. *Consumers' Research Magazine* 77 (5) (May 1994): 18–23.

Wecht, C. H. Patient access to medical records: Yea or nay? *Legal Aspects of Medical Practice* (October 9, 1978): 8–10.

Waller, Adele A., and Oscar L. Alcantara. Ownership of health information in the information age. *Journal of the American Health Information Management Association* 69 (3) (March 1998): 28–34.

Zemet, Nan. The knee bone's connected to . . . ? A guide to medical resources for those with little or no medical background. *Legal Assistant Today* (May/June 1996): 56–63.

Zemet, Nan. Unlocking the secrets of medical charts. *Legal Assistant Today* (September/October 1994): 68–72.

Zick, Colin J. Legal aspects of medical records confidentiality. *Journal of the American Health Information Management Association* 66 (5) (May 1995): 57–62.

Index

About the Author

CHARLES C. SHARPE is a retired pediatric clinical nurse specialist. In addition to his many years of experience in clinical nursing practice, the author has been a faculty member of the departments of nursing and paralegal studies in several colleges in southeastern Pennsylvania. He is also the author of *Nursing Malpractice: Liability and Risk Management* (Auburn House, 1999).

www.ingramcontent.com/pod-product-compliance
Ingram Content Group UK Ltd.
Pitfield, Milton Keynes, MK11 3LW, UK
UKHW020813290926
15470UKWH00003B/1126

9 780865 692831